THE KING OF ROME

Borgo Press Books by CHARLES DESNOYER

Joan of Arc: A Play in Five Acts
The King of Rome: A Play in Five Acts (with Léon Beauvallet)

ALSO OF INTEREST:

Napoléon Bonaparte: A Play in Five Acts, by Alexandre Dumas

THE KING OF ROME

A PLAY IN FIVE ACTS

CHARLES DESNOYER &

LÉON BEAUVALLET

Translated and Adapted by Frank J. Morlock

THE BORGO PRESS
MMXII

THE KING OF ROME

Copyright © 2001, 2012 by Frank J. Morlock

FIRST BORGO PRESS EDITION

Published by Wildside Press LLC

www.wildsidebooks.com

DEDICATION

For my only son, Miles, with love

CONTENTS

CAST OF CHARACTERS 9
PROLOGUE, Scene 1 11
PROLOGUE, Scene 2 27
ACT I, Scene 3 57
ACT II, Scene 4 85
ACT III, Scene 5 113
ACT III, Scene 6 117
ACT III, Scene 7 119
ACT III, Scene 8 122
ACT IV, Scene 9 141
ACT V, Scene 10 159
EPILOGUE, Scene 11 182
EPILOGUE, Scene 12 183
ABOUT THE AUTHOR 184

CAST OF CHARACTERS

EMPEROR NAPOLEON (I)

MARSHALL BERTHIER

DOCTOR YVAN, Doctor to the Emperor

MICHEL LAMBERT, also as MATHIAS WERNER

FIRST USHER

SECOND USHER

MADAME ROBERT

A LADY OF HONOR

NAPOLEON (II), KING OF ROME, DUKE OF REICHSTADT (aged 17-21)

THE GHOST OF NAPOLEON (I)

ABBÉ ORSINI

BARON DE RHEINFELD

PRIME MINISTER

ARCHDUKE CHARLES

INFANT OF PORTUGAL

JOSÉ, his factotum

THE DOCTOR, Doctor to the Duke of Reichstadt

BIRMAN, The Duke's valet

FOUR CONSPIRATORS, friends of Michel Lambert

JEANNE Muller, a young orphan adopted by Michel Lambert

PROLOGUE, 1811 - 1814
SCENE 1. THE CANNON OF THE INVALIDES

The Tuilleries, March 20, 1811. A room. In the back a balcony giving on a garden. Entry doors left and right. Marshall Berthier is conversing with a Lady of Honor. Diverse groups of general officers and ladies. Michel Lambert, grenadier of the imperial guard is on duty by the entry door at the right.

LADY OF HONOR:

Well, Marshall, what news from outside? What are the feelings of the Parisian population?

BERTHIER:

The same as ours, Madame! The nation associates itself heartily with the great idea of its sovereign! It sees itself reigning and triumphing in him. And the heir that he demands, it knows is for itself a guarantee of its future glory and security.

LADY OF HONOR:

Oh! May his hopes and ours be realized.

MICHEL LAMBERT:

(aside) We will have a son, that's certain. A Little Emperor, nothing less!

BERTHIER:

Oh how many wishes, how many wishes at this moment for and against!

LADY OF HONOR:

What are you saying? All France wants a son.

BERTHIER:

France, yes! But Europe? What is its thought? Who can tell?

MICHEL LAMBERT:

(aside, laughing) Europe! We must get its permission right away, excuse us! (the door opens at the right and two ushers appear)

USHER:

(announcing) The Emperor!

(Napoleon enters, everyone moves aside and bows as he passes. The Emperor is pale; he seems exhausted with fatigue and emotion. He bows without speaking and sits at the right. From the Emperor's entrance, Michel Lambert remains motionless before the door. Deep silence.)

NAPOLEON:

(after a long silence, turns) Hello, gentlemen. (noticing Berthier)

Hello, Berthier!

BERTHIER:

(bowing) Sire!

NAPOLEON:

(moved) Your hand! Your hand, my old friend!

BERTHIER:

(coming forward and pressing Napoleon's hand) You are upset, Sire?

NAPOLEON:

Upset! Yes! I spent the night with the Empress! Poor woman. I wept. I wept for the first time!

MICHEL LAMBERT:

(drying his eyes) Come on, good! Here I am crying, too! (The Emperor goes to the window and looks out for some time in silence)

NAPOLEON:

They are all there! Awaiting with impatience for the cannon to sound and announce to the world whether the dynasty of Napoleon must perpetuate itself or die out. (he walks up and down with agitation) Oh, a son! a son! I will have one! The prayers of the people are a sure guarantee of it. Today, especially, their love for me is revealed in its entirety. For them I am no longer the conqueror, the triumpher, I am not coming, brow covered with laurels, from Wagram and Austerlitz; no—

no dazzling success, no intoxicating battle, my only title to their good wishes and prayers is my love for that child who does not yet exist, and who absorbs in me all the joys of victory, all the pleasures of triumph. (turning to Berthier)

BERTHIER:

(advancing) Sire!

NAPOLEON:

What are they saying in Paris?

BERTHIER:

All the churches are filled with an enthusiastic crowd which mingles your name with its prayers.

NAPOLEON:

Yes! I know the people love me. They share my joys, my hopes, as they share my sorrows. Ah, if you knew, friend, what my anxiety has been since yesterday. Each hour that passes is a century for me! Don't think, friend, don't think that a vain personal ambition makes me demand a son! No, no. My ambition is noble and great! When carried by the French people on the imperial shield I accepted the mission which was confided to me; I took an oath to accomplish it! Well, a bullet can carry me off; a knife blow will suffice to stop me in my path; at my death my victories are lost, my works nullified, my plans of reform and civilization impossible. I want to leave this heritage to my son. I intend that after me, the suffering people shall find in him a tireless defender. I intend that the old order, sapped by me in its foundations, will collapse entirely beneath his efforts, swallowing all those privileges of ignorance, all those stale doctrines, all those abuses of absolutism, and that in the midst of these ruins, surging to the voice of the son of Bonaparte, a new world, regenerated and palpitating with enthusiasm, patriotism and truth—

DOCTOR YVAN:

(entering from the right) Sire! Sire!

NAPOLEON:

Doctor! Why this concern? This agitation?

DOCTOR YVAN:

Sire, a great danger threatens the Empress.

NAPOLEON:

What are you saying?

DOCTOR YVAN:

To save the child and the mother at the same time may be impossible.

NAPOLEON:

Impossible! Above all, my God! Above all, save the mother! Come, come, Doctor!

(Napoleon leaves quickly followed by Doctor Yvan. General consternation.)

BERTHIER:

O dreams of the future? What's become of you now?

LADY IN WAITING:

My God! My God! Save the Empress. (she kneels at the back, as do all the ladies)

MICHEL LAMBERT:

(resuming his station) That's all the same! None of all this will prevent us from having a little Emperor.

BERTHIER:

What are you saying?

MICHEL LAMBERT:

I say, my Marshall, that the child will live or my name's not Michel Lambert, that's all!

BERTHIER:

You are crazy!

MICHEL LAMBERT:

Excuse me, my Marshall, I am known in the regiment to enjoy a wit as lucid as it is penetrating, as penetrating as it is—

BERTHIER:

You're mad, I tell you. Shut up.

MICHEL LAMBERT:

I'm shutting up, my Marshall. (aside) But not thinking any less. We will have a little Emperor!

(At this point a cannon shot is heard. The women get up and everyone listens with the greatest anxiety, Berthier is with Michel Lambert near the door.)

MICHEL LAMBERT:

(to Berthier) Pardon, excuse me, my Marshall! I don't know if my ears deceive me, but it seems to me I just heard a cannon shot?

BERTHIER:

Indeed! (second cannon shot)

MICHEL LAMBERT:

Another one! Ah! Ah! It would appear that old Michel spoke the truth, and that the imperial eaglet has just been born.

BERTHIER:

(agitated) Listen! (third cannon shot)

MICHEL LAMBERT:

Number three! Just ninety-eight to go, and the count will be correct.

BERTHIER:

And not to receive any news! (cannon shot)

MICHEL LAMBERT:

There, my Marshall. That makes four.

(Everyone listens. The door opens and the usher appears.)

USHER:

(announcing) The Baron de Rheinfeld, envoy from the court of Austria. (Rheinfeld enters and bows) The Abbé Orsini, envoy from His Holiness.

MICHEL LAMBERT:

(aside) Come on, good! Kings and Jesuits. Indeed, all can lend a hand. (cannon shot) Five! There it goes.

(The Abbé enters and everyone bows; the Abbé seems to bless them.)

ABBÉ ORSINI:

May the peace of the Lord be with you, my brothers.

MICHEL LAMBERT:

And may the Devil from hell confound you, good father!

(Cannon shot. Everyone again lends their attention to the exterior noise; Michel Lambert counts on his fingers. Baron de Rheinfeld and Abbé Orsini are talking.)

BARON DE RHEINFELD:

Well, Abbé? What do you think of all this?

ABBÉ ORSINI:

I think! First of all, I think we must be prudent, and that we are alone in our opinion here.

BARON DE RHEINFELD:

(shaking) Huh?

ABBÉ ORSINI:

That's the cannon from the Invalides! It won't thunder long. Twenty-one guns, no more. I prayed for that all night. (cannon shot)

MICHEL LAMBERT:

(continuing to count each shot as it comes) Eight!

ALL:

(repeating) Eight.

BARON DE RHEINFELD:

Why, look here, Abbé, look here! One cannot say whether that cannon is announcing life or death? (cannon shot) Decidedly it's irritating.

MICHEL LAMBERT:

Here, there is dancing down there! It cannot be said it is the effect of French cannons on Prussians, Russians and other dogs of that species. (cannon shot) Ten! It's long in coming! but that's all right! It's going to come!

ABBÉ ORSINI:

Ah, Baron! What joy I will experience to see that man's pride take a fall.

BARON DE RHEINFELD:

Today, perhaps, goodbye to his dynasty, if it pleases Heaven to send him a girl instead. (another cannon shot) Ten more and it will be all over.

MICHEL LAMBERT:

Another Ninety and Long Live France.

ABBÉ ORSINI:

The French people are fascinated by the constant luck of Bonaparte, and will turn against him when they see fortune abandons him; when all hope of a dynasty becomes illusory. (cannon shot) After today, Baron, let's try to profit by the general discontent, by sowing hate of the sovereign among the people and scorn for his authority. Our fortunes depend on the success of our negotiations. Think of it carefully, Baron.

BARON DE RHEINFELD:

I am thinking of it.

ABBÉ ORSINI:

The reward of your services will be the Chamberlain's key.

BARON DE RHEINFELD:

And yours, a Cardinal's hat.

ABBÉ ORSINI:

A Cardinal. That's what I'll be. (cannon shot; The Abbé shudders)

MICHEL LAMBERT:

Cursed Italian. He has a shifty, pettifogging air about him. He gives me the impression of a devil. (cannon shot) Fifteen. Ah! Ah! It's warming up.

BARON DE RHEINFELD:

Abbé!

ABBÉ ORSINI:

What do you want?

BARON DE RHEINFELD:

Suppose our foresight was false?

ABBÉ ORSINI:

What do you mean?

BARON DE RHEINFELD:

If, instead of a girl— (cannon shot)

ABBÉ ORSINI:

Impossible! Heaven doesn't wish it. Hasn't Bonaparte dared to proclaim everywhere that he will give to his future offspring the title of King of Rome!

BARON DE RHEINFELD:

The King of Rome! (cannon shot)

ALL:

Seventeen.

ABBÉ ORSINI:

(continuing) That title belongs to our Saint Peter, the Pope! So it's an assassination of his temporal power and God won't permit it.

BARON DE RHEINFELD:

You reassure me. (cannon shot) Ah, indeed, that will never end!

MICHEL LAMBERT:

Eighteen.

ALL:

Eighteen!

MICHEL LAMBERT:

Eighteen. Eighteen. (cannon shot)

ALL:

(anxiously) Nineteen.

ABBÉ ORSINI:

Well, Baron, what's the matter with you? You are pale as a dead man!

BARON DE RHEINFELD:

You think so! Why no, why no, I am calm and certain. (cannon shot)

MICHEL LAMBERT AND THE OTHERS:

Twenty!

BARON DE RHEINFELD:

I confess I am deeply moved.

ABBÉ ORSINI:

Moved! Moved! See here, Baron, you would get a saint damned!

BARON DE RHEINFELD:

What do you want, my pious friend? It's stronger than I am. It's much stronger— (a cannon shot interrupts his thought) than I am!

ALL:

(with great emotion) Twenty-one!

(A great silence.)

ALL:

Nothing more.

MICHEL LAMBERT:

Nothing more. We've counted wrong, that's certain.

ABBÉ ORSINI:

(overwhelmed with joy) Well, you see, Baron, it's a girl!

BARON DE RHEINFELD:

It's a girl. I'll have my key.

ABBÉ ORSINI:

I get my hat. Your health, Chamberlain.

BARON DE RHEINFELD:

Your health, Cardinal.

(A cannon shot, much louder than all that preceded it.)

ABBÉ AND BARON:

(stupefied) Huh!

MICHEL LAMBERT:

Come on; I really knew it was coming.

USHER:

(announcing) The Emperor!

NAPOLEON:

(entering) Well! Gentlemen, we have a big lad! He had to be dragged by the ear a bit, but at last he's come.

(There's a general shout, both within and without, while

Napoleon goes to the balcony to greet the people.)

PEOPLE:

(outside) Long Live The Emperor! Long Live the King of Rome!

NAPOLEON:

(on the balcony) Thanks, thanks, gentlemen. Ah, this day is the most beautiful of my life. (Baron de Rheinfeld and Abbé Orsini come to bow before him)

BARON DE RHEINFELD:

Sire, I lay at your feet the homage and congratulations of the European powers.

ABBÉ ORSINI:

And as for me, I bring to the Prince Imperial the blessings of the father of the Church.

NAPOLEON:

Thanks, gentlemen, thanks! For a long while I've known the feelings of Rome towards me. I receive the wishes of Saint Peter and those of all the sovereigns of Europe. I appreciate all their frankness, and I count on soon thanking them again myself in their palaces.

MICHEL LAMBERT:

(aside) Famous! I will be there. Crush the Jesuit and (shouting with all his might in the ears of the Abbé and the Baron who are near him) Long Live the Emperor! Long Live the King of Rome!

(The shouts of the people mix with those of the characters on stage. Napoleon once again shows himself at the window.)

ALL:

Long Live the Emperor! Long Live the King of Rome!

(The Curtain falls.)

CURTAIN

PROLOGUE
SCENE 2. THE CHILD KING

The action takes place on January 23, 1814. A ground floor room on the same level as the gardens.

USHER:

(entering with Madame Robert at the back) That's fine, Madame, that's fine. I am in charge of your petition. (she gives it to him)

MADAME ROBERT:

And you will deliver it to him, sir?

USHER:

Or at least, I will have it delivered to him.

MADAME ROBERT:

Oh, let him read it. My God, let him read it and I am saved.

USHER:

(opening a door at the right) Go in here and wait! Be careful that no one notices your presence.

MADAME ROBERT:

I promise you that. (she disappears and shuts the door)

USHER:

Marvelous. Here's the duty officer.

MICHEL LAMBERT:

(enters singing from the left, he wears the epaulettes and uniform of a lieutenant, he's in dress uniform, cross of honor, etc.)

Ah, if loves take root
I will plant it in my garden
I will plant it all over
So I can share it
With my comrades!

(noticing usher) A subordinate in dress.

USHER:

(aside) He's in a good mood, fine! (aloud) My Lieutenant.

MICHEL LAMBERT:

Well?

USHER:

I've something to ask of you?

MICHEL LAMBERT:

Speak, I'm listening.

USHER:

You're on duty today?

MICHEL LAMBERT:

So the rumor runs.

USHER:

You are going to see Marshall Berthier?

MICHEL LAMBERT:

Evidently that is likely.

USHER:

Then I beg you, be good enough to deliver this to the Emperor through his intermediary. (presents him with the petition)

MICHEL LAMBERT:

Again! Ah, indeed, today it's raining petitions.

USHER:

Reassure yourself, it's still the same one.

MICHEL LAMBERT:

What? It's that brave woman! Come, I don't wish to be harsh. Give it to me, young man. (the usher gives it to him)

USHER:

And do you think that the Marshall—?

MICHEL LAMBERT:

The Marshall! Heavens, is there something he could refuse me, who campaigned with him in Russia and Germany?

USHER:

Ah, that's different, from the moment that—

MICHEL LAMBERT:

Yes, young man, it's as I have the honor to tell you. I didn't leave him for a minute, for three consecutive years. Indeed, from the day our little king came into the world.

USHER:

The 20th of March, 1811!

MICHEL LAMBERT:

It's as you said, conscript! And during those years, I earned all my promotions, one after the other, under his command. Up to, and including, Lieutenant. I covered him and myself with laurels of every kind.

USHER:

I was unaware of that, my Lieutenant.

MICHEL LAMBERT:

By Jove, young man, there are many chapters in the history of France that you are unaware of.

USHER:

Here's the Marshall.

MICHEL LAMBERT:

That's good, leave us. I'm going to softly insinuate the thing in question. (the usher leaves by the right)

BERTHIER:

(entering from the rear) Ah! Ah! It's you, Michel!

MICHEL LAMBERT:

Myself, my Marshall. Ready to serve you, if I am capable of it.

BERTHIER:

(wanting to take Michel's hand and noticing the petition he's holding) What's that?

MICHEL LAMBERT:

My Marshall—that's something for you.

BERTHIER:

For me?

MICHEL LAMBERT:

Actually, no!

BERTHIER:

No!

MICHEL LAMBERT:

Actually, yes!

BERTHIER:

Are you crazy? Let's see. Explain yourself.

MICHEL LAMBERT:

The fact is, this is a petition.

BERTHIER:

(shaking his head) The Devil! At this moment—

MICHEL LAMBERT:

My Marshall! It's a service to render to a poor woman.

BERTHIER:

(a little impatient) Come on, give it to me. (Michel delivers it to him)

USHER:

(at the left, announcing) The Emperor!

MICHEL LAMBERT:

I am making myself scarce, and I am counting on you, my Marshall. (leaves by the rear)

NAPOLEON:

(entering without seeing Berthier; he holds a paper in his hand and says with rage) Conspiracies! again! always! Civil war, when foreign wars come to assail us on all sides. When tonight, this very night, it's necessary to leave to repulse the foreigner who threatens us. Civil war! That's their war, these Royalists! Let all France perish and become slave or Cossack, so long as they regain their privileges and their royal puppet.

BERTHIER:

(aside) The moment is not very favorable.

NAPOLEON:

And above all that, traitors around me! Political time servers without heart and without conscience. Twisting always to the side of those who will buy them. Yesterday for the Republic, today for the Emperor, tomorrow for Royalty. But always, and above all for themselves and themselves alone. Ah! such men! Let's not think of them any more, I need to be calm. (to one of the ushers) Advise the Empress that I am going to pass by her apartment; I want to embrace my son.

BERTHIER:

(deciding to speak to him and presenting the petition) Sire!

NAPOLEON:

Ah, it's you, Berthier. What do you want?

BERTHIER:

(hesitating) Sire, before leaving this room would you cast your eyes on this paper—

NAPOLEON:

(taking it) This paper. What is it?

BERTHIER:

A petition, Sire!

NAPOLEON:

(returning it to him angrily) I don't want it. Take it back, Marshall, take it back, and I don't want to hear any more about it!

BERTHIER:

Sire!

NAPOLEON:

Enough, I tell you, enough! A petition. Truly, this passes all belief! What! Our frontiers are occupied by foreign troops, the whole of France is suffering and trembling, and there exist hearts cold enough not to understand such calamities.

BERTHIER:

Sire—

NAPOLEON:

(with severity) All individual suffering must disappear. All private interest must cease, all egoism must be silent before these sole words:

Danger to the Fatherland.

BERTHIER:

Sire, a woman!

NAPOLEON:

Again! To dwell on this subject is to disobey me! I intend that in the future all solicitors will be kicked out of the palace.

SECOND USHER:

(returning) Sire, Her Majesty, The Empress is ready to receive you.

NAPOLEON:

My wife, my child. Ah! I need your caresses to distract me from the thoughts that are burning my heart. (leaves by the rear, followed by the usher)

BERTHIER:

(alone, enraged) May hell confound all petitions and petitioners!

MICHEL LAMBERT:

(appearing gaily at the back) I saw the boss leave. Let's accost the Marshall!

BERTHIER:

(with anger) Ah! Ah! It's you.

MICHEL LAMBERT:

Myself, my Marshall. Well, the petition?

BERTHIER:

(returning it to him with fury) Here it is! From now on address yourself to others. I am not in any mood to play that game again.

MICHEL LAMBERT:

(stupefied) Huh? huh? Marshall?

BERTHIER:

Go away! Enough!

MICHEL LAMBERT:

Still, Marshall—

BERTHIER:

(furious) Eh! By Jove! Go to the Devil. (leaves by the rear)

MICHEL LAMBERT:

(furious, striding up and down silently, then stopping, exasperated) Go to the Devil! (the usher comes in silently and taps him on the shoulder; Lambert turns, still furious) Go to the Devil!

USHER:

(recoiling) Huh!

MICHEL LAMBERT:

(advancing on him) You and all ushers, past, present and future.

USHER:

(terrified) But, Lieutenant—

MICHEL LAMBERT:

(hurling the petition to the ground) There! There's your petition. May it burn your fingers!

USHER:

(advancing) Lieutenant, I think—

MICHEL LAMBERT:

(taking him by the arm and turning him around) Again! Come on. A half turn to the right, Pekinese, or beware the—

USHER:

(stupefied) Pekinese!

MICHEL LAMBERT:

Go to the Devil! (leaves by the left)

USHER:

(rubbing his arm) Pekinese!

MADAME ROBERT:

(quietly opening the door at the right) He's alone! Sir! (the usher turns)

USHER:

(bitterly) It's you.

MADAME ROBERT:

Well, sir, my request?

USHER:

(getting more and more enraged) Here it is! Take it back, Madame, take it back, and never bring it again.

MADAME ROBERT:

(gathering it up) But, sir—

USHER:

But Madame, I am able to do nothing for you. Nothing in the world. Leave, leave, you must and as fast as possible and don't come back.

MADAME ROBERT:

Leave! Without a response! Without a word of hope!

SECOND USHER:

(announcing) The Emperor!

USHER:

(to Madame Robert) Leave! Leave! You've got to. (he leads her to the door at the right and she disappears) Just in time!

(Everyone comes in with the Emperor, whose anger has vanished completely. Michel Lambert is a few steps behind.)

NAPOLEON:

(exalted) The Future— You still belong to me! My son's caresses have restored my strength and confidence! Come, Kings of Europe. Yesterday you were at France's knees, today you unite against her. At my voice, the whole country is going to rise up. Come and we will crush you, you and that pack of slaves you drag in your suite! (sitting down, left) Berthier.

BERTHIER:

Sire!

NAPOLEON:

I received you harshly just now. What do you want? An access of somber bitterness carried me away! Now I am calm and I recognize my wrongs. Do you pardon me for them?

BERTHIER:

(bowing) Ah, Sire.

NAPOLEON:

Thanks. (thumbing through papers and taking notes)

BERTHIER:

(to Michel) Michel.

MICHEL LAMBERT:

(very frigid) My Marshall.

BERTHIER:

I addressed some words to you.

MICHEL LAMBERT:

A little sharp, it's true.

BERTHIER:

Well, if I beg you to forget them, will you remain bitter toward me?

MICHEL LAMBERT:

Bitter. Ah, indeed, excuse me. With you, my Marshall?

BERTHIER:

(offering him his hand) So, it's finished?

MICHEL LAMBERT:

(taking his hand) It's dead and buried! (going to the usher and tapping him on the shoulder) Eh! Young man!

USHER:

(trembling) Lieutenant.

MICHEL LAMBERT:

Lieutenant Michel has to tell you that his intention was not to molest you, he consents to give you his hand, if you like, if you don't like, he'll sock you in the eye, that's all!

USHER:

(enchanted) Ah, Lieutenant, from the moment your intention was not—you must understand that mine is not. Your hand, Lieutenant. (they shake hands)

MICHEL LAMBERT:

Funny bipeds, all the same, these ushers.

MADAME ROBERT:

(softly opening the door at the right, trembling) He's here!

USHER:

Heavens, the petitioner! As for me, I'd forgotten her.

MADAME ROBERT:

I am trembling—

USHER:

(aside) Poor woman! (going to her) I was a little abrupt just now. Everyone has his bad moments and I ask your pardon for it.

MADAME ROBERT:

Ah, sir.

NAPOLEON:

(turning to Berthier) Marshall!

BERTHIER:

Sire!

NAPOLEON:

Well, what about that petition?

BERTHIER:

(embarrassed) The petition, Sire? (Madame Robert quickly gives it to the usher who gives it to Michel Lambert)

MICHEL LAMBERT:

(low to Berthier) Here's the object.

NAPOLEON:

(still seated) Well?

BERTHIER:

(giving it to him) Here it is.

NAPOLEON:

(reading the address) Well— Why, it's not for me. It's addressed to the King of Rome!

BERTHIER:

(astonished) The King of Rome? (exchange of looks between the characters)

NAPOLEON:

In the end, I am still the tutor of His Majesty; his kingship is no more than a regency, and I am the Regent. (giving the petition back to Berthier) Read!

BERTHIER:

(reading) "Sire, your father, The Emperor, has such grave occupations that sometimes it can happen that he forgets—" (Berthier stops)

NAPOLEON:

Well! Keep reading.

BERTHIER:

(resuming) "—forgets the misfortunes and services of some of his subjects—"

NAPOLEON:

(frowning) What's this mean?

BERTHIER:

(looking reproachfully at Michel) I am unaware!

MICHEL LAMBERT:

(glaring at the usher) I'd forgotten. Pekinese.

USHER:

(repressing anger and looking at Madame Robert) I don't remember any more.

MADAME ROBERT:

Ah, I am dying of fright.

NAPOLEON:

(rising and taking center stage) Give it to me! (after Berthier gives him the petition, he resumes reading with ill humor) "Your father, The Emperor has such grave occupations that sometimes he may forget the misfortunes and services of his subjects."

(Silence. New ricochets of ill right up to Madame Robert who supplicates the usher, who in turn supplicates the Lieutenant, right up to the Emperor.)

NAPOLEON:

(resuming reading) "You, at least, Sire, will have the time to listen to my prayer and you won't reject it. I implore your kindness for a child of your age. A poor girl, whose mother has been dead for a month of starvation and sorrow, and whose father Jacques Muller, Captain of The Old Guard, died two years ago in the service of France at the crossing of the Beresina!" (general emotion, Napoleon notices Madame Robert) The Beresina! Oh, what a memory. What a memory. (silence) But, this letter must be delivered to my son!

MADAME ROBERT:

(timidly) I already did, Sire!

MICHEL LAMBERT:

I put it in his hands.

USHER:

And I read it aloud to him.

NAPOLEON:

Ah! And what did he reply?

MICHEL LAMBERT:

Nothing!

USHER AND MADAME ROBERT:

Nothing!

NAPOLEON:

(looking at them, smiling) Well—silence is consent!

MICHEL LAMBERT:

Indeed, I didn't think of that.

NAPOLEON:

The King of Rome gives a pension of four thousand pounds to the daughter of Captain Muller. She will be raised at Saint Denis, in the midst of the children of my brave companions in arms. (general joy)

MADAME ROBERT:

Ah, Sire, you are great and good!

SECOND USHER:

(announcing) The King of Rome!

(A squad of Grenadiers forms in the back; the King of Rome passes in a little open carriage pulled by goats. Several ladies of the palace follow with pages.)

NAPOLEON:

(raising Madame Robert, who is still kneeling, and saying to her with emotion) Go, Madame! Go thank my son. The poor girl you took up in pity is henceforth under his protection. Pray Heaven that he one day may not be orphaned as she is.

(Madame Robert walks towards the back and bows; the child extends his arms to her and embraces her, then she leaves. Michel Lambert moves away as well. One of the ladies of honor pulls the child out of his carriage and leads him to the Emperor.)

NAPOLEON:

Give him to me, give him to me, Madame. And leave him with me. I want him to be mine alone during these last hours that I must spend near him. (to Berthier) Marshall, do everything to prepare for the departure.

(Everyone leaves. All the doors are shut. Napoleon takes the child in his arms and sits with him on the couch at the right, fixing lovingly the child's hair, while the child plays with Napoleon's epaulettes and decorations, then little by little falls asleep.)

NAPOLEON:

Dear child. Desire of my days past, hope of my future. You, poor angel, whose long curly hair I so love to kiss; I've got to leave you, to deprive myself of your caresses. If it were forever— (the child is in a deep sleep, Napoleon takes some papers and glances over them exactly as in Steuben's picture) Tomorrow I will be very far from you, and perhaps—

FIRST USHER:

(entering from the left) The Envoy of His Holiness asks Your Majesty the favor of an audience.

NAPOLEON:

(surprised) Show him in! The Pope's Envoy at this juncture. What can he want from me?

USHER:

(announcing) The Abbé Orsini. (the Abbé enters, the Usher leaves)

NAPOLEON:

(still seated) Would you excuse me, Abbé? Allow me not to interrupt his sleep, and let him repose on my knees while listening to you. (pointing to an armchair at some distance from him)

ABBÉ ORSINI:

Sire, in the name of His Holiness, I come to offer you the prayers and the intervention of the Church with the Allied powers.

NAPOLEON:

The intervention of the Church!

ABBÉ ORSINI:

Say one word, and the armies which threaten the frontiers on all sides are going to withdraw; this campaign which can only be disastrous for you won't take place. Do you wish it?

NAPOLEON:

And what does His Holiness ask as the price of solicitude?

ABBÉ ORSINI:

The title of King of Rome was given by you to your heir.

NAPOLEON:

Well?

ABBÉ ORSINI:

Well, Sire, we ask you to renounce for your son that title which is a denigration of the rights of the Church.

NAPOLEON:

Its rights!

ABBÉ ORSINI:

(raising his voice) They've been recognized for all time by Europe and His Holiness pretends to just title—

NAPOLEON:

(interrupting him coldly) Lower, I beg you, much lower. Sir, the King of Rome is sleeping—

ABBÉ ORSINI:

(rising) I understand, Sire, a refusal.

NAPOLEON:

Formal and irrevocable. (rises and after having gently placed the child's head on a cushion, resumes) As I see it, France has done much more for the Pope than it ought to have done. It's time that Saint Peter proclaimed the reforms that our treaty imposes on him! It's time he distanced himself from all these perfidious advisors, all these Tartuffes with miters who are leading him to his ruin and intend to deliver Italy to the rapacity of the Austrians! Finally, remind Saint Peter, Abbé, that the Concordat allies him to France.

ABBÉ ORSINI:

(handing him a parchment) Well! Here's what breaks that alliance.

NAPOLEON:

What's that?

ABBÉ ORSINI:

A note from the Pope, which retracts the Concordat. You want war, Sire, you will have it!

NAPOLEON:

(proudly) Much lower, sir, much lower, the King of Rome is sleeping. (reading the Pope's note and hurling it to the ground, scornfully) War. I accept it! Just fine; I haven't forgotten the murders of Verona, and Napoleon must avenge the soldiers of Bonaparte murdered in the name of religion. I will do it!

ABBÉ ORSINI:

Your Majesty is really resolved to break with the Church?

NAPOLEON:

With those who prostitute it and dishonor it; with those who, using its name, order massacres, and who speak to nations with a cross in one hand and a dagger in the other. Those I hate and I scorn. Go, sir. Go take my reply to Saint Peter.

ABBÉ ORSINI:

(bowing) Sire, I pray to Heaven for you. And for your child. (he leaves)

NAPOLEON:

(repeating with emotion the Abbé's last phrase) I pray to Heaven for you and for your child! That Jesuit will bring me misfortune. (an usher enters at the back)

USHER:

The Duty Lieutenant.

MICHEL LAMBERT:

(entering with a package) Sire, telegraphic dispatches.

NAPOLEON:

Ah! It's you, Lieutenant Michel Lambert. Give them to me.

MICHEL LAMBERT:

Here, Your Majesty. (aside, joyful) He recognized me.

NAPOLEON:

(reading) "The Austrian army has just penetrated the borders of France and it's headed towards Troyes! The city is in danger. Brienne is in the power of the Russians. The Castle is defended by the Prussians! Montmerail, Montereau, Champ-Aubert are occupied by the Allies—" Already! Already! Foreigners on the soil of France! My child! My child! (looking at his son, he dries a tear)

MICHEL LAMBERT:

The Emperor is upset! Those brigands of Allies! That emotion will cost them dear. (moves to the left, leans on the couch)

NAPOLEON:

(getting control of himself) Huh! What are you saying? You saw me weeping, Michel. Ah! Don't tell anyone you saw Napoleon weeping!

MICHEL LAMBERT:

No, no, my Emperor. But I understand those tears. You are thinking of your son, as I am thinking of—

NAPOLEON:

Of whom?

MICHEL LAMBERT:

A poor little girl—

NAPOLEON:

Ah! You're a father?

MICHEL LAMBERT:

Not precisely; but it's all the same.

NAPOLEON:

How's that?

MICHEL LAMBERT:

I've just adopted an orphan girl. You just now, your pensioner, or rather, his— (pointing to the King of Rome) the little girl with the petition.

NAPOLEON:

The daughter of Captain Muller.

MICHEL LAMBERT:

A former comrade. I too, like My Little Emperor, I wanted to do something for her. And I've sworn to serve as a father to the poor child—

NAPOLEON:

(looking at the King of Rome) And as for me—as for me, if I've embraced him today for the last time—

MICHEL LAMBERT:

The last time! For goodness sake, what are you saying, my Emperor?

NAPOLEON:

Who would serve him as a father?

MICHEL LAMBERT:

Damn! I am really a small thing, Majesty, compared to all those you've made generals, Marshalls, Kings of Sweden and the whole shivering lot. But if, in default of all those folks, you don't turn your nose up at a poor soldier who dreams of nothing in the world but you and (pointing to the child) him—with France included, of course, and my little orphan girl. I would swear, indeed, that I will give to that child the last drops of my blood—whatever may happen!

NAPOLEON:

Fine, my brave man; I accept your offer.

MICHEL LAMBERT:

And I will keep it, my Emperor! As well, perhaps, better than a Marshall of France.

(Napoleon embraces him; Berthier, generals and officers enter, followed by the ladies of the court who surround the couch where the King of Rome is sleeping.)

NAPOLEON:

(to Berthier) Well, Marshall—is everything ready for departure?

BERTHIER:

Everything is ready, Sire.

NAPOLEON:

Come gentlemen, come everyone. France is invaded! The world is watching us and the nation calls us. Let us answer it with a unanimous spirit. Let's make for it this sacrifice of our riches and our affections. Nothing for us! Nothing for us! Everything for France!

GENERAL SHOUT:

Everything for France!

NAPOLEON:

(to the officers of the National Guard) You, Gentlemen, and you also, Michel. The Empress and the King of Rome are under your protection.

MICHEL LAMBERT:

And we will defend them to the death.

OFFICERS:

(swords extended towards the couch) To the death! (military music in the garden)

NAPOLEON:

(listening) Ah, the joys of the family; the happiness of being a father— All that is suspended today, lost perhaps. (to Michel Lambert) Tell them, tell them to play another tune. Stand and Salute the Empire!

MICHEL LAMBERT:

Yes, Majesty. (he disappears, then returns and mixes with the other officers)

NAPOLEON:

(embracing his son) Perhaps I'll never see him again! (with effort) Goodbye! Goodbye! Enough of being a father, we must be a soldier! Let's march, gentlemen, let's march.

(The ladies have picked up the King of Rome. Michel Lambert carries him in his arms. The child sends kisses to his father.)

ALL:

Long Live the Emperor!

NAPOLEON:

(taking off his hat, solemnly) Gentlemen— Long Live France! (casting a last look at his son, he puts himself at the head of his generals and officers)

(The band plays "Stand and Salute the Empire.")

CURTAIN

ACT I
SCENE 3. THE DAUGHTER OF A SOLDIER

The action takes place in 1828, fourteen years after the last scene in the prologue. The stage represents a country view. To the right, the entrance of an inn of poor appearance. Tables here and there. In the back, trees. In the extreme distance, little houses and a village clock. Tables right and left in front of the inn.

AT RISE, the Abbé Orsini and Baron de Rheinfeld enter and cross the stage, looking attentively at the inn.

ABBÉ:

(pointing to the inn.) Here! Here it is!

BARON:

Here? In this wretched inn?

ABBÉ:

Yes, baron.

BARON:

This frightful hovel?

ABBÉ:

Precisely. It's in this direction that our young student heads every time he attempts to escape you.

BARON:

Oh! That happens so seldom!

ABBÉ:

Very seldom, indeed. Every day for the last month.

BARON:

Huh? Why, that's impossible! Your Eminence must—

ABBÉ:

Don't call me Eminence! When young, I coveted the grandeurs of the Church and the Cardinal's cap! I obtained it fourteen years ago, after the fall of Napoleon, but today of all vanities, I wish to be and am, nothing.

BARON:

Nothing, except the dear confidant, the intimate friend, the soul of His Excellency the Prime Minister, who directs the Emperor, or nearly does, Monsignor.

ABBÉ:

No Monsignor! I am the Abbé Orsini, nothing more. I repeat to you that our student, The Duke of Reichstadt, comes here every day! This frightful hovel, as you call it, contains for him, a treasure.

BARON:

A treasure!

ABBÉ:

A young girl!

BARON:

Ah, a girl of the people, a wench. By Jove, I've seen some very pretty wenches.

ABBÉ:

A simple peasant girl who's been living here for the last three months with her father, the old innkeeper, and her beauty creates an uproar in the country! Our young man is in thick with the innkeeper, and even better with—

BARON:

With the daughter. I understand. The kid is a handsome lad—he resembles—

ABBÉ:

Silence.

BARON:

He resembles the one the Holy Alliance forbids us to name!

ABBÉ:

Especially before him—who must remain for a long while ignorant of the name of his father.

BARON:

Ah! He's in love already! Seventeen years old, and your plans for him, Abbé, your hope to make a holy man of him—one of the lights of the Church?

ABBÉ:

A dream. Of the conqueror's heir I was hoping to make a monk, and now this cursed love—

BARON:

And that's her, without a doubt—

ABBÉ:

Who?

BARON:

The wench! She's charming.

(Jeanne, in an elegant German peasant's costume, comes out of the inn.)

BARON:

The kid doesn't have bad taste.

ABBÉ:

Silence. And support me, Baron.

BARON:

That's agreed.

JEANNE:

(looking around her) He's not here. (she utters a scream of surprise, finding herself surrounded by the two diplomats) Ah!

ABBÉ:

(severely) My child. Don't forget the paternal advice I gave you. Your love is sinful.

JEANNE:

Sinful!

BARON:

It's infamous. It's an atrocity.

ABBÉ:

And Heaven cannot fail to punish you.

JEANNE:

Heaven! But I swear to you, sir—

ABBÉ:

I will add that, before the celestial rage, you will have others to worry about. Here, Baron. Make her understand, in the least gentle way possible!

BARON:

Don't worry! I know how to embellish a thought, however violent, by choice of statement. (going to Jeanne) Miss, when a woman of the people allows herself to debauch the son of a family—she gets locked up.

ABBÉ:

You understand—

JEANNE:

Ah! That terrifying word. (going into the inn, calling) Father! Father!

ABBÉ:

He's not coming. Without doubt, he has other business—

JEANNE:

(aside) Heavens, I'm dying of fright.

ABBÉ:

We will leave you! Weigh our words. They are heavy.

BARON:

Although softened by the artifices of language.

ABBÉ:

But they are true! Don't forget them!

JEANNE:

(to herself) Oh, never!

(The Abbé and the Baron move away into the back.)

JEANNE:

(alone, frightened, watching them leave) No. I cannot forget them. These terrible threats, these outrageous reproaches that I have not deserved, and yet they strike me to the heart. The son of a family? Him, Frantz, oh! If that is true, my God, I don't ask to see him again. And, I will be happy if he never comes back here. (turning towards the back) Ah, that's him. Perhaps—no, no, the friends of my father. Those whose mysterious visits make me uneasy for him.

(First one peasant enters from the right, then another from the left. Then, from different sides, two groups of two persons. Two others of three. All sit at different tables, at a certain distance from each other, and seem not to know each other. Then, one of the men rises and goes into the inn.)

JEANNE:

Yes, they come from all sides. And, there they are, not saying anything, taking seats at different tables, then one of them goes to warn my father! What's all this signify? I don't know, but when the priest told me just now "He isn't coming. Doubtless he has other business—" I shivered. For it seems to me that the man in black, who knows my secret, has also penetrated the secret my father is hiding even from me.! Here he is!

(Mathias Werner, who is none other than Michel Lambert, returns with the man who went to fetch him.)

MICHEL LAMBERT:

That's fine comrades, that's very fine. The friends are faithful to the rendezvous. I'm expected there! (to Jeanne) Well! What are you doing, my child? When you stay there to look at me like a spectacle? Leave us. I have a word or two to say to my old acquaintances while cracking a crust and swallowing a glass of wine. Well—get going!

JEANNE:

Yes, Father. (aside) I'm going to find out about all this. (goes back into the inn)

MICHEL LAMBERT:

(in a low voice as he serves the different tables) Marvelous! Each at his post! (to the men at the back table) You, there. You're on watch. At the first suspicious face you notice, yell loud for some wine!

FIRST PEASANT:

(at back) And rapping the table.

MICHEL LAMBERT:

That's it. And we will stop. I will only be the old Austrian innkeeper and you all—

SECOND PEASANT:

Drunks from the same country.

MICHEL LAMBERT:

That's it. Perfect. Drunks and first of all, to get into the spirit of things: To your health! (taking a glass)

ALL:

(clinking and drinking) To yours!

MICHEL LAMBERT:

To the success of our enterprise! (sitting down; they all group around him except those at the back) It's working! I have news from Paris, Rome and Milan. Excellent. Everywhere friends, points of support. One thousand of ours. Old guards. There are not many generals and Marshalls among them, that's true. Those rabbits are too rich; above all they want to save their skin. But a thousand soldiers and officers of the Empire are ready to support the swift works that, you and I, comrades, must strike at Schoenbrunn.

SECOND PEASANT:

To reach him! That's what's necessary.

THIRD PEASANT:

The Duke of Reichstadt!

MICHEL LAMBERT:

My little Emperor! I can't get used to calling him anything else.

JEANNE:

(who's just reappeared in the doorway, repeating emotionally) The Duke of Reichstadt! (she remains hidden and eavesdrops on the others by the half-closed door)

SECOND PEASANT:

(to Michel) But haven't you seen him yet?

MICHEL LAMBERT:

Where at? They have good gates at Schoenbrunn—and walls, too.

THIRD PEASANT:

But they assure us that recently they've given him a bit more freedom, and sometimes, alone, incognito, he escapes from the palace.

MICHEL LAMBERT:

I don't believe it! Incognito! Would I be mistaken? I who knew him by heart, before having seen him. I would recognize him in a thousand—and never!

FIRST PEASANT:

(shouting and rapping his stein very hard on the table) Some wine! Some wine! Eh, old gossip of a father Mathias, we are asking some wine of you.

MICHEL LAMBERT:

Coming! Coming. (rushing to the back, jug in hand)

(At the same time he looks toward the right, toward the exterior, and the peasants do as well. Jeanne takes a step forward and looks past them towards a very young man dressed in a black coat who stops to greet the innkeeper.)

JEANNE:

(with emotion) Ah! It's him, it's Frantz!

MICHEL LAMBERT:

(greeting the young man) Hello, hello, Mr. Frantz! You are not stopping for a moment at my inn!

FRANTZ:

No, no, Papa Mathias! Not right now. I will return.

MICHEL LAMBERT:

Goodbye!

FRANTZ:

(addressing himself to the girl rather than to the old man) Goodbye!

JEANNE:

(aside) Ah, for the first time, the sight of him made me feel bad. (she goes into the inn and shuts the door, Frantz leaves)

MICHEL LAMBERT:

(watching the young man leave, while talking to his friends) A child; a little student I've taken a liking to, even though he is an Austrian. I've even promised to teach him fencing and the charge at double time. He takes me for an old Austrian soldier and he adores me; as for me, I find him a good lad, but I only tell him what I want him to know.— He's far enough away, let's return to our business!

FOURTH PEASANT:

To The Duke of Reichstadt.

MICHEL LAMBERT:

I was telling you that I would recognize him in a thousand; but I haven't had the chance. Fortunately, I am not easily discouraged and I don't complain of my difficulties or my actions! For the moment, under the name Mathias Werner, I am soliciting a situation as a gardener in the palace and I hope to obtain it through Archduke Charles, the uncle of the young prince!

SECOND PEASANT:

Known. The one who commanded the Austrian army at

Wagram; I saw him!

ALL:

And I, too, I, too!

MICHEL LAMBERT:

That's right! A brave soldier who adores his nephew, from the way it appears, and who, alone is worth more than all of his family. I will see him, possibly as soon as today.

ALL:

Today?

MICHEL LAMBERT:

Yes! I have intelligence in the palace. I need a protector near His Highness, a protector at all hours, at all moments, and if I cannot have him for free, I will buy him!

ALL:

Buy?

MICHEL LAMBERT:

A little expensive! For me at least. Four thousand francs.

ALL:

Four thousand francs!

MICHEL LAMBERT:

Just that much! A year of the pension that the Emperor gave, in the name of his son, to my adoptive daughter and which has been paid to us faithfully since the fall of the Empire, by the mother of Napoleon, the ancestress of all the Bonapartes! (the door opens, Jeanne reappears and walks towards Michel without being noticed by him or those who surround him; Michel continues) That sum, in happier times, I will return to Jeanne!

JEANNE:

No, father.

(General surprise. All recoil and utter exclamations.)

MICHEL LAMBERT:

Jeanne! You were there? You were listening?

JEANNE:

Don't you think me worthy of hearing you? That sum which you have disposed for such an enterprise, I don't want to be returned to me by you nor by anyone; and that's not all. I want my share in your dangers, I want that. And if I could ever manage to reproach you, it would be for having doubted either me or my courage! I am the daughter of a soldier! And I owe everything, you just said it, to he who died at Saint Helena!

MICHEL LAMBERT:

(excitedly) Lower! Lower! My daughter!

JEANNE:

Yes, you're right, father; but promise me, won't you, to do me the honor in the future, and put me in the midst of your plans?

MICHEL LAMBERT:

(rising and embracing her) Come on! Good blood cannot lie! Give her your hands, comrades; she won't betray you any more than I. (he sits down) Today, I count on seeing the Archduke. Birman, his valet de chamber, whose good graces I've purchased at your expense, my daughter, has given me a meeting at noon. He must deliver to me my letter of audience, and tomorrow, perhaps, I will have my place in the palace.

JEANNE:

And mine, father?

MICHEL LAMBERT:

Yours, too, my child. Can I separate from you? (to peasants) You, friends, wait, wait still. Patience before audacity. The Gardener of Schoenbrunn may really be able to open the gates to you. Who knows?—one day.

ALL:

One day?

MICHEL LAMBERT:

Let's not talk about it. Perhaps it's only a dream. But a little expedition in the manner of the Isle of Elba would deucedly do my business and yours, right? (all shake his hand) Soon, comrades.

(They leave in different directions.)

ALL:

Soon!

MICHEL LAMBERT:

(pulling out his watch) Eleven thirty! It will take me only ten minutes to go to the palace! But first of all, I ask your pardon, my little Jeanne, for the adventurous life to which you are condemned and the perils I cast before you!

JEANNE:

I'm expecting them and when I began to suspect them, it was for you alone I trembled, father; but I no longer worry about them, since I must share them with you. Also, I must tell you that this excitement is necessary to my life. It will make me forget him.

MICHEL LAMBERT:

Forget— Forget who?

JEANNE:

Him!

MICHEL LAMBERT:

Who's him?

JEANNE:

(pointing to the back) That young man you just saw here a moment ago. The one to whom you offer your hand every day.

MICHEL LAMBERT:

Ah! Damn! Blind man that I was. Frantz. The little student, you love him?

JEANNE:

I love him!

MICHEL LAMBERT:

And for how long?

JEANNE:

Since the first day I saw him.

MICHEL LAMBERT:

Wait— The 4th of last October.

JEANNE:

Yes, father, the day of the feast of Saint Francis. At the ball you took me to in the clearing of the forest.

MICHEL LAMBERT:

I remember, by Jove. The celebration for the old Emperor! I had to play my role as a faithful German, of a good and sincere Austrian! And then, I told myself that a ball in any country in the world ought to please a young girl! And it's there that—

JEANNE:

That I saw him, yes, father! Alone, isolated from everyone;

he seemed foreign to the burning joy which exploded around him. His eyes were full of boredom and sadness, which I saw animate when fixing on mine! Since then, he's never left me. And as for me, even with lowered eyes I always saw him, and I saw only him! He approached me and invited me to a waltz! I don't know why I should have wanted to refuse, but I didn't have the strength to answer. I felt the hand he offered me shake in mine and—and the orchestra had just played the prelude to the dance! It was—I haven't forgotten anything—the tune you love so much, father—because it was composed by him—him—you know whom I mean!

MICHEL LAMBERT:

Ah! The tune from the Waltz of the Duke of Reichstadt!

JEANNE:

That's it. He told me I was the most beautiful girl at the ball; that I had just appeared to him like an angel of solace and goodness, and that if he were never to see me again my image would never be effaced from his soul. I listened. He spoke to me very low. And despite the uproar of the music I didn't lose one of his words; and can you believe it, father? I didn't see that along with him, I was dragged into the whirl wind of that waltz! When everyone around us stopped to applaud and admire us! From the moment he saw all the gazes of that enthusiastic crowd directed at us, he escaped me, saying very low. "Till tomorrow!" I didn't understand what I was experiencing, and what new thought had just seized all my being. But I couldn't forget him. Absent, I still saw him; finally it seemed to me that my life, henceforth was inseparable from his.

MICHEL LAMBERT:

And the next day?

JEANNE:

And the next day, it was with you that I saw him again. He'd made you his friend, father, and since that day you haven't stopped praising him to me.

MICHEL LAMBERT:

That's true! It's my fault, my little Jeanne. It's very much my fault! That lad pleased me when I compared him to all these German blockheads. I found pleasure in talking with him, drinking with him. Youth! Something generous! A good child. Something French, yes, something French in his character? He suits me. He suits me a lot this little greenhorn. But dammit all, he doesn't any more. He doesn't suit me at all any more! Talk to you of love! and under my nose, under my beard!

JEANNE:

And sometimes, also, father, in your absence.

MICHEL LAMBERT:

In my absence! Ah, bah! He dared.

JEANNE:

You leave me so often, my good father!

MICHEL LAMBERT:

You're right! You always are. Always my fault. And Heavens, in the midst even of that ball you've reminded me of, I wasn't thinking of you. I was with my friends. Those who just left us! And I was only living for our enterprise. Oh, but don't worry, now I am no longer blind. And I will keep all of my duties before me at once. And first of all (pointing to the left) that's the way he left just now. I am going to find him on my way. As happens every morning. And I will treat him—like the Austrian he is! Ah, indeed, say, now I think of it—

JEANNE:

Of what, father?

MICHEL LAMBERT:

Because on your side you aren't going to defeat my work. For, after all, you told me that you love him.

JEANNE:

I don't love him any more. He deceived me—a son of a family.

MICHEL LAMBERT:

Ah, bah! That's all we need: liar and seducer! At his age! There are no children any more! Oh, I'll get my hands on him.

JEANNE:

I hate him.

MICHEL LAMBERT:

I will execrate him. So much the more do I adore my little Emperor. I will return my daughter, embrace me! (kisses her face and leaves by the left)

JEANNE:

Finally I am alone! And my father won't see these tears. The last! I have too much pride in my soul to keep his memory after what I have just learned.

FRANTZ:

(entering gaily from the left) He didn't see me, that dear Mathias!

JEANNE:

Ah! It's him!

FRANTZ:

Myself, Jeanne. I, who am unable to resist my impatience, and who just carefully avoided the sight of your father to get to you more quickly.

JEANNE:

Sir—

FRANTZ:

Oh! Don't scold me! I love him! I really love him, that excellent Mathias! But you mustn't hold it against me, if I love you more, you, who are, henceforth, all my happiness, all my life.

JEANNE:

Stop, sir. These words?

FRANTZ:

Well, are you really surprised to hear them, Jeanne? And especially, don't you believe them?

JEANNE:

No, sir, no. I no longer believe them! For it's not through you, I know who you are!

FRANTZ:

Who I am! (aside) Ah, my God—she knows. Then she's going to tell me. (aloud) What, Jeanne—you've learned?

JEANNE:

A single thing. That we must be strangers to each other.

FRANTZ:

Who told you that? Who could lie in this way? Strangers to each other. Why, before knowing you, Jeanne, I wasn't living; I had neither belief in myself nor the instinct for those great and beautiful things that must make us adore life; the instinct for love and glory! I was unaware of all that! I didn't know you. A meeting at a ball, a glance from you, a word of conversation with you and your father who spoke to me of war and battles, I guessed everything. I realized I was not born for the brutishness of the monastery, and I had but two thoughts, two desires, two passions in the world: I wanted to be loved by you, Jeanne, and I wanted to be a soldier!

JEANNE:

Be a soldier and may your dreams of glory be accomplished! Loved by me! No longer hope for that! Your family—

FRANTZ:

Ah! You know it? They told you—

JEANNE:

They told me that your family was rich and powerful.

FRANTZ:

That's all?

JEANNE:

That's all. Isn't that enough?

FRANTZ:

Then you are unaware that this rich and powerful family, it's true—treats me like a disinherited child. That, it hides from me with obstinacy even the name of my father, as if it were a cause to blush for him? That secret, what is it? Funereal and wretched without doubt, since they've resolved to withhold it from me! And it's I, perhaps, who mustn't dare say I'm your equal, you a daughter of a soldier. But answer me, Jeanne, if your birth was a thousand times above mine would you think yourself abased in offering me your hand?

JEANNE:

Oh—you can't be thinking of it, sir?

FRANTZ:

Well, this mystery which weighs on my life—I'll penetrate it. And whatever it may be I will tell you everything, happy or unhappy, weak or powerful. I will confide to you all my secrets, to you who I honor as much as I love. At last, my dear Jeanne. (he takes her hand; Jeanne withdraws it carefully seeing the Abbé and The Baron reappear on the right)

JEANNE:

Oh, Heaven!

FRANTZ:

What's the matter with you?

JEANNE:

It's them!

FRANTZ:

(to himself) My governors! (aloud) You know them?

JEANNE:

I know from them that I must reject your love.

FRANTZ:

What? What did they say to you?

JEANNE:

Oh, words I'm ashamed to repeat.

FRANTZ:

In short?

JEANNE:

(in a low voice) That, when a girl of the people allows herself to debauch the son of a family, they lock her up.

FRANTZ:

Oh the wretches! Why, I will round on them! (the Baron and the Abbé cross the stage; Frantz glares at them and continues) Yes, I'll round on them, and if all the earth is opposed to my love, I will struggle against the whole world.

MICHEL LAMBERT:

(enters from the left and hears these last words; he has a paper in his hand) And against me, Mr. Frantz.

JEANNE:

(terrified) My father.

FRANTZ:

(gaily) Against you, too, my dear Mathias! (offering him his hand, Michel withdraws)

MICHEL LAMBERT:

I am no longer your dear Mathias!

FRANTZ:

Indeed!

MICHEL LAMBERT:

Not at all. And I beg you never to set foot in my inn again.

FRANTZ:

I shall return.

MICHEL LAMBERT:

Despite me?

FRANTZ:

Despite you, if need be!

MICHEL LAMBERT:

I forbid you to do it!

FRANTZ:

All the more reason.

MICHEL LAMBERT:

Think carefully. I have a will.

FRANTZ:

And so do I. I will return tomorrow, not later.

MICHEL LAMBERT:

Tomorrow!

FRANTZ:

And we will understand each other, I am sure of it. And like yesterday, you will call me your friend, you will see.

MICHEL LAMBERT:

Never, never, I tell you!

FRANTZ:

Always, always! My old Mathias! Till tomorrow, Jeanne, till tomorrow. I will love you all my life. (leaves excitedly)

MICHEL LAMBERT:

All his life. Oh, I am in a rage. (strides about furiously)

ABBÉ:

(holding his arm) Don't be uneasy! He won't come back and you are under our protection.

MICHEL LAMBERT:

Huh!

BARON:

Have no fear, we shall protect you, goodman, we will.

MICHEL LAMBERT:

(to himself) Goodman? (on this word, his paper falls from his hand as the Baron and the Abbé leave by the right) (watching them) Now those are two horrible phizes. The Devil take me, it seems to me I've already seen them.

JEANNE:

Father, relatives without doubt!

MICHEL LAMBERT:

Relatives of his? All the more reason for me to get my hands on him, if he's got ingrates like that in his family! Let him come back, and I will prove to him I am master in my own home, I am—

JEANNE:

(picking up the paper from the ground) What's this paper?

MICHEL LAMBERT:

Ah, I was forgetting; my letter of audience! Quick, my daughter: to Schoenbrunn.

JEANNE:

I am ready.

MICHEL LAMBERT:

I shall have my situation, and you will be sheltered from the pursuit of this little Austrian seducer.

JEANNE:

Yes, father; I won't see him any more.

MICHEL LAMBERT:

(giving her her hat and cloak) Never. Let's leave, my daughter, and may Saint Napoleon protect us.

BOTH:

Let's leave! Let's leave! (they walk toward the back)

CURTAIN

ACT II
SCENE 4. THE INFANT OF PORTUGAL

The stage represents the Schoenbrunn palace, in a ground floor gallery with gardens to the left, a prieu Dieu to the right by a table covered with books and papers. In the back, right a stairway leading to the palace. The Archduke Charles is seated at the table, Birman, his valet, is standing near him.

BIRMAN:

I have the honor of reminding Your Highness that he intended to grant an audience.

ARCHDUKE:

To your protégé, Mathias Werner and his daughter. That's fine, I will receive them.

BIRMAN:

Here, milord?

ARCHDUKE:

Yes, in this oratory! I don't wish to be far away. (aside) I don't know what plans they are hatching against my poor Frantz; I will be here to defend him.

BIRMAN:

(announcing) The Abbé Orsini; the Baron de Rheinfeld.

ARCHDUKE:

Ah! Those men! Let's control myself and not let them see how much I hate and scorn them.

(Both enter and bow to the Archduke, who casually returns their bows.)

ARCHDUKE:

Well, Gentlemen, what news? What has His Excellency the Prime Minister decided on the subject of the Duke of Reichstadt?

ABBÉ:

Can Your Highness be unaware of it? His Majesty himself did not tell you?

ARCHDUKE:

The Emperor! I am excluded from those councils to which you are admitted, sir. So speak, I beg you! What's happening? What are the wishes of the Prime Minister? Or rather, what are yours?

ABBÉ:

The Emperor alone has the right to decide about this! His Majesty and I am going to announce this to my colleague Baron de Rheinfeld. His Majesty, dating from today, is withdrawing the education of the young prince from us.

ARCHDUKE:

What are you saying?

BARON:

Dismissed! (aside) What an injustice!

ARCHDUKE:

Gentlemen, you cannot be expecting compliments or condolences from me. You know quite well, I've never approved the wretched education you've inflicted on the son, to punish the glory of the father. But, by whom are you being replaced?

BARON:

Indeed. By whom?

ARCHDUKE:

Do you know, Abbé?

ABBÉ:

Perfectly, Milord. The choice of His Majesty falls on a proscribed noble who has found a generous hospitality in the Court of Vienna. On a royal prince, on the heir of Braganza and Alcontia—The Infant of Portugal.

ARCHDUKE AND BARON:

(together) The Infant of Portugal!

ARCHDUKE:

(with rage) Such a wretch! A monster that the King, his father, drove out of Lisbon for his infamous crimes and debaucheries! And this is the preceptor that you and yours wish to give my nephew!

ABBÉ:

But Milord—

ARCHDUKE:

But sir, I no longer beg you, and I am not doing you the honor of discussing it with you! Who? Him! That man! The murderer of Beni Posta imposed as guardian, as master of the Duke of Reichstadt! Ah, all my heart is revolted at that thought. I am going to find the Emperor. He will drive that man from the Court or I will leave myself! (he goes out by the back)

ABBÉ:

He'll leave! Indeed, that's what I was hoping for.

BARON:

His Imperial Highness is right; he speaks admirably.

ABBÉ:

By approving their pass over of you?

BARON:

No, indeed! But he's right about that which concerns the new governor of our student.

ABBÉ:

Be silent, Baron—

BARON:

But—

ABBÉ:

Shut up! To accept a disgrace without complaint is the proper thing for a man of intellectual character

BARON:

(excitedly) Then I'm not complaining.

ABBÉ:

The nomination of The Infant of Portugal by His Excellency the Prime Minister is one of those caprices of a statesman that even those that he includes most in his thinking cannot approve of without reservation, but which will perhaps be justified by success! As to the rest, his installation delivers us from the Archduke Charles. Let's try to accept it with good grace and to efface ourselves before him! You especially, Baron, be silent. I repeat: they passed over you, but without destroying you. You will keep your honorariums.

BARON:

Really? My honorariums? Honor is satisfied! I ask nothing more.

BIRMAN:

(announcing at the back, left) His Royal Highness, The Infant of Portugal. (both remove their hats)

ABBÉ:

(to the Baron) Come on, act until the end like a man of character. Do your successor the honors of the situation he has just taken from you!

BARON:

Wouldn't it be better, Abbé, that you yourself, as a man of character—

ABBÉ:

Not at all! I have nothing to give to him. It's your affair.

BARON:

Pardon, it's yours—

ABBÉ:

Yours!

INFANT:

(smiling, low) Poor folks—they won't speak to me! It costs them to address me their congratulations. I am going to extract some pain from them. (aloud) Gentlemen, I receive with pleasure the statement of your devotion and sympathy. I will be worthy of it. I have only one desire:

that's to justify, in the duties in which I am called to succeed you, the alacrity and enthusiasm that you demonstrate in offering them to me.

ABBÉ:

(aside) The insolent!

BARON:

(aside) He's laughing at us.

INFANT:

You had, didn't you, my dear colleagues, to communicate to me your ideas on the steps I must take in the education of my cousin?

BARON:

(low to the Abbé) His cousin.

ABBÉ:

(low) Doubtless. Between royal families.

BARON:

(low) That's true. They are all cousins even when they dethrone each other!

INFANT:

But your silence proves to me that you have confidence in me. You make fine, very dear, very excellent colleagues! My duties: here they are: To serve above all the plans of Europe: to destroy this young man who could one day become so formidable; to choke his budding illusions. Never to tell him anything except that which is judged incapable of awakening in him any idea of greatness or ambition. But often, and this is a special concern, that your gravity prevented you from taking, often to remind him he's no longer a child and to permit him all the pleasures of his age, to dispense them to him even with a certain largess, to weaken him and make him sleep in the delights of Capua! Baron, you who taught him history, you understand.

BARON:

Perfectly! (aside) Vice and orgy are going to replace devotion.

ABBÉ:

(to Infant) You said, Milord, that for such a ministry a special sort of man was required, and they would not have thought of me to fill it.

BARON:

As for me, I would have tried it! One does what one can. (bowing) Milord, certainly—

INFANT:

My dear colleagues, I receive the new statement of your wishes and—

BARON:

And all our sympathy.

ABBÉ:

(to himself) Decidedly, this is an error of the Prime Minister; God alone is infallible.

(The Baron and the Abbé leave by the right. The Infant sits down nonchalantly to the right.)

INFANT:

(to a man at the back) José.

JOSÉ:

(coming forward) Milord!

INFANT:

Everybody here detests me.

JOSÉ:

I was afraid of that.

INFANT:

Except for one person who is the master of the whole world.

JOSÉ:

His Majesty.

INFANT:

No, His Excellency.

JOSÉ:

The Prime Minister.

INFANT:

I don't need anyone except him! And if I properly fulfill his views relative to my cousin, The Duke of Reichstadt, it's he who will one day give me the crown of Portugal!

JOSÉ:

(shrugging) The crown—

INFANT:

Rejoice, my good José, my faithful barber, my inseparable, the companion of my exile and my adventures. You with whom I've always shared everything.

JOSÉ:

Shared everything. But keeping the lion's share for yourself, milord. And leaving me that of—

INFANT:

(rising) Poor José.

JOSÉ:

To you the pleasures, to me the fatigue duty. To you good luck, to me blows and kicks. (gestures of kicking) You've got the front, and I've got the reverse of the medal; indeed I am not the companion, but the butt, the suffering pain of Your Highness.

(The Infant has stopped listening. He turns his back and goes upstage. Michel Lambert and Jeanne appear in the back, accompanying Birman)

INFANT:

Oh! Caraco! How pretty she is.

JOSÉ:

Don't swear, Milord! And morality, chastity. You owe your student an example.

INFANT:

My student—poor fellow. You understand nothing of His Excellency's program.

BIRMAN:

(introducing Michel and Jeanne) Would you wait in this oratory? His Highness, The Archduke is in secret conference with His Majesty. (coming forward with them and finding himself near the Infant, who is observing Jeanne very closely, he bows) Ah, pardon, Milord. I didn't see Your Highness.

MICHEL LAMBERT:

That! A Highness! This jackal's head!

BIRMAN:

Bow, bow indeed! The Infant of Portugal.

MICHEL LAMBERT:

Indeed, the Infant of Portugal. (bows to the Infant, and Jeanne makes a curtsy)

INFANT:

(moving away and observing the young girl through his lorgnette) José! If she's an inhabitant of Schoenbrunn, I'll say a few things to her.

JOSÉ:

(low) Watch out! The old man doesn't look easy— I....

INFANT:

That's your concern.

JOSÉ:

Come on, good, my backside. I will never escape it. (they leave together)

MICHEL LAMBERT:

You need more than a crown to embellish a face like that.

JEANNE:

(to herself) His look froze me with horror!

MICHEL LAMBERT:

(looking around him emotionally) Finally, we are here. Schoenbrunn, my promised land! I am here and I won't die without seeing him! him! my other child! my little Emperor! Goodness—what.

JEANNE:

(to herself, looking around her like her father) From now on, by giving myself to the plans of my father, to the deliverance of the Duke of Reichstadt, I shall have the strength to forget Frantz.

MICHEL LAMBERT:

(questioning Birman during the proceeding lines) This room!

BIRMAN:

The oratory and study of the young Prince. (they run their eyes over the furniture as Birman continues) There. His music papers. His books. His designs.

MICHEL LAMBERT:

(pointing to the left) And that?

BIRMAN:

His prieu-dieu.

JEANNE:

(pointing to a missal, covered by a box in velour engraved with the Imperial insignia and placed on the prieu-dieu) This book?

BIRMAN:

His book of hours.

JEANNE AND MICHEL:

(together) Ah!

MICHEL LAMBERT:

(aside) I've something better than that for him.

BIRMAN:

(looking outside) Milord, the Archduke is leaving the apartment of His Majesty. I am going to warn him of your arrival.

(Birman disappears into the Park. Jeanne takes the book of hours and looks at it with emotion.)

MICHEL LAMBERT:

(watching a guard who, since the beginning of the act, has been patrolling the gate at the rear and who disappears from time to time) Give that to me, my child. (Jeanne gives him the book of hours) Ah! That soldier has stopped looking at us. (pulling the book from its box)

JEANNE:

What are you doing? (Michel returns the missal to Jeanne, and pulls from his breast another book, which he places in the box) Ah, I understand.

(Jeanne places the missal on the console to the left. Michel Lambert replaces the cover on the prieu Dieu, just as the sentinel reappears; then Birman announces the Archduke.)

BIRMAN:

His Imperial Highness, Milord The Archduke.

ARCHDUKE:

(entering and looking at Michel and Jeanne who bow to him) Mathias Werner, isn't it?

MICHEL LAMBERT:

Yes, Milord. (aside, looking at him) That's him! That's really him!

ARCHDUKE:

Huh! What are you saying?

MICHEL LAMBERT:

Nothing, Milord. (again to Jeanne) He's indeed the one we beat at Wagram!

ARCHDUKE:

(impatiently) Again!

MICHEL LAMBERT:

Absolutely nothing.

ARCHDUKE:

Well, that's exactly my answer to you, on the subject of the request you've addressed to me.

MICHEL LAMBERT:

What, Milord. My position at the Château—

ARCHDUKE:

Impossible.

JEANNE AND MICHEL:

(together) Impossible!

MICHEL LAMBERT:

Your Highness refuses—?

ARCHDUKE:

I do not refuse. But The Archduke Charles no longer has the power to protect anyone here!

MICHEL LAMBERT:

What do you mean?

ARCHDUKE:

(to himself, crossing the stage with agitation) The Emperor has given way to the Prime Minister. He extends his hand to this Portuguese. And me, as for me, I am invited to spend some months on my estates.

MICHEL LAMBERT:

Milord, I beg you—

ARCHDUKE:

Useless! I am leaving the court this very day, and I only have time to embrace my nephew! Ah, here he is! (goes back toward the right)

JEANNE AND MICHEL:

(together) Here he is!

MICHEL LAMBERT:

(low) Ah, at last, for a moment, one single moment, I will see him.

JEANNE:

Over this way! Over this way, father.

(They hurry towards the place the Archduke has been with his nephew, but at that moment the guard reappears and bars their way.)

SENTINEL:

Get back.

BIRMAN:

(coming down the stairway) You've got to leave!

MICHEL LAMBERT:

(low to Birman) But it seems to me—!

BIRMAN:

But, it's my instruction. Do you want to ruin me? You've got to leave.

MICHEL LAMBERT:

(pushed by Birman) Not even to see him! Now there are four thousand francs well placed.

(Michel Lambert and Jeanne are pushed towards the left as the Duke and the Archduke appear on stage by the stairway at the right.)

DUKE OF REICHSTADT:

(dressed as before, with the addition of a star of diamonds on his breast) What are you telling me, uncle? You're leaving?

ARCHDUKE:

Instantly.

DUKE OF REICHSTADT:

You, my support; the only one in this palace to whom I can open my soul. You are abandoning me?

ARCHDUKE:

They demand it! I am banished from Schoenbrunn!

DUKE OF REICHSTADT:

Banished! You uncle? Is it really possible?

ARCHDUKE:

(to himself) The wretches! What are they going to do to him?

DUKE OF REICHSTADT:

But I will see my grandfather, the Emperor. He loves me. I will persuade him to let you stay near me, or at least to let me leave with you.

ARCHDUKE:

With me? Take care they don't grant it to you. It's because of you they are exiling me.

DUKE OF REICHSTADT:

Eh! Why, uncle?

ARCHDUKE:

Why? (aside) The Devil! I've said too much. I must get away. I am so furious I will say even more. (aloud) Goodbye! Goodbye!

DUKE OF REICHSTADT:

Oh, stay. Stay longer! Look, we are not reduced to such a degree of abasement that a valet from the Prime Minister dares approach you to rush your departure! They will give you plenty of time to embrace me. And as for me, time to say goodbye to you, uncle.

ARCHDUKE:

(holding him in his arms) My friend, my poor Frantz!

DUKE OF REICHSTADT:

(sitting at the right) So, it's really true? Because of me? I bring bad luck to all those that I love! And what a day they chose to tear you from my love. Never, perhaps, was it more necessary for me to see you, to speak to you, to confide my secrets to you!

ARCHDUKE:

Ah! What? You've got new ones?

DUKE OF REICHSTADT:

(rising) Yes, uncle. I love; I am loved. And I've sworn she will be my wife!

ARCHDUKE:

Your wife! Who is she?

DUKE OF REICHSTADT:

She!

ARCHDUKE:

She! She! That's not a name.

DUKE OF REICHSTADT:

Ah, uncle, if you knew her—

ARCHDUKE:

Eh, if I knew her, and if you were four years older, and if you were still heir to a throne, it's not I who would have the right to marry you together! As for you, yourself—they wouldn't consult you.

DUKE OF REICHSTADT:

Why?

ARCHDUKE:

Your wife! That doesn't concern you nor me at all!

DUKE OF REICHSTADT:

Why—

ARCHDUKE:

It's an affair that must be decided by all Europe.

DUKE OF REICHSTADT:

But still—why?

ARCHDUKE:

Ah! Why! (aside) That word with him is my continual terror! And despite myself, I am still afraid of answering.

DUKE OF REICHSTADT:

Europe! Europe does me too much honor! Europe. Let it tell me then who I am to at least justify the importance it accords me, and the slavery to which it forces me to submit.

ARCHDUKE:

(aside) Ah. Now we are there.

DUKE OF REICHSTADT:

No, look, uncle, it's time to put an end to all this uncertainty. I want at last, I intend to know myself! I am nothing. And if they exile you on account of me. I am nothing and I cannot dispose of my hand, of my heart, without the consent of all Europe! Answer? Why all these eternal contradictions? Why?

ARCHDUKE:

(aside) Always! Always that word! I've given my word and I won't fail in it on the day of my disgrace. (aloud) Goodbye! Goodbye! my friend— (wants to leave)

DUKE OF REICHSTADT:

You are fleeing me. Why?

ARCHDUKE:

Yet another why? Heavens! I can no more reply to this than to all the others! Goodbye, Frantz, goodbye! (he leaves by the left; The Duke sits on the terrace)

DUKE OF REICHSTADT:

I remain confounded. He, my only friend, my only hope! he is silent and he is leaving. (looking out he sees the Infant appear) Ah! There's this new governor, this tyrant. Less than that; this spy, they are imposing on me. (rises)

INFANT:

(coming and bowing to him) Milord! I hope that Your Highness will not have to regret—

DUKE OF REICHSTADT:

Let's shorten it, sir. From our first interview, I propose to state briefly what your situation is towards me, and mine towards you! I think you are not qualified to teach me anything, that it remains for me to learn! I submit then to your presence, but I do not accept any lessons. I am, determined, do what they may—to be my own master. I don't know what tells me; I am born, rather to command than to obey!

INFANT:

(in a low voice) Indeed, and I, too!

DUKE OF REICHSTADT:

You are saying?

INFANT:

I'm saying that one can say, without shame, that he has for his governor the heir to a crown!

DUKE OF REICHSTADT:

What does that matter to me? A crown. The question is having the right to wear it.

INFANT:

And do you intend, Milord, reversing the roles and becoming

preceptor in your turn—do you pretend to teach me how to wear it?

DUKE OF REICHSTADT:

Why not? I sense I have enough reason and energy for that. I have an instinct for all the glories to which a prince can give a noble impulse; like that of all the miseries he is called upon to console! (gesture by the Infant) Yes, sir—I will give you lessons, perhaps; in courage, humanity and justice.

INFANT:

(aside) Justice! This character will disgrace the monarchy. Happily, he will never mount a throne. (The Duke, impatient of the Infant's presence mechanically wanders about the stage. He stops before the prie-dieu, taking up the book for a moment. Then, rejecting it, he marches towards the table and sets to writing. To himself) What's he doing? How moved he seems as he writes. A love letter, perhaps! Oh caraco! If it were possible!

DUKE OF REICHSTADT:

(speaking as he writes) Jeanne!

INFANT:

(to himself) Jeanne!

DUKE OF REICHSTADT:

(continuing) Poor girl, you are again going to accuse me of having deceived you. I was counting on the support of my uncle and I hoped that tomorrow— (continues writing)

INFANT:

Oh. Very certainly, it's a love letter.

DUKE OF REICHSTADT:

(rising after having sealed it) No one! No one to confide myself to. (pacing with agitation)

INFANT:

(aside) I am going to recover the good graces of my pupil. (aloud, going to the Duke) Milord, since you're Seventeen and I'm Twenty-five—! It's true I cannot be a governor for you, in all seriousness at least. Both young and both princes, you almost in prison, as for me, suddenly exiled. It's better for us to understand each other than to seek a quarrel.

DUKE OF REICHSTADT:

Understand each other!

INFANT:

I must gain by it, Milord. You cannot lose by it.

DUKE OF REICHSTADT:

Explain yourself.

INFANT:

At bottom, we understand absolute royalty in the same manner! I intend to be—to the letter—the father of all my subjects! For I wish to be especially adored by their wives and their daughters, which tells you that I understand the restlessness and impatience that you are experiencing at this moment. And that I desire to put an end to it! Nothing easier than to send that letter to its address! (calling) José! José!

DUKE OF REICHSTADT:

What are you doing?

INFANT:

A man in my confidence that I am putting at your orders. Among the instructions given me by the Prime Minister, I don't have that of intercepting such correspondence.

(Night gradually begins to fall.)

DUKE OF REICHSTADT:

But, sir—

INFANT:

(still calling) José!

JOSÉ:

(coming from the palace) Here I am, Milord.

INFANT:

Then get here, wise guy, when you are called! (to Duke) I repeat to you, milord, this man is yours!

DUKE OF REICHSTADT:

(aside) He's more despicable than I could have believed.

INFANT:

I think he's beginning to appreciate me more!

DUKE OF REICHSTADT:

(aside) After all, what does the messenger matter? I have to see her, I have to speak to her; she will at least know that I haven't forgotten her, and that I will never forget her. (throws purse to José, then hands him the letter)

JOSÉ:

(taking the purse and the letter) Ah, Milord. (reading the address) The Black Eagle Inn, I know it. I'm going there. (aside) I face all sorts of catastrophes! I've got compensation in advance. (he leaves)

(Lackeys enter the stage from different sides, bearing lighted candles and shutting the drapes at the back. Religious music. The clock strikes.)

DUKE OF REICHSTADT:

Ah! The evening prayer!

ABBÉ:

On your knees! On your knees and let's ask Heaven to grant many years to our august sovereign. (he prays; all the characters kneel)

DUKE OF REICHSTADT:

(opening the prayer book) The History of Napoleon Bonaparte!

ABBÉ:

(the only one standing, dominating all the characters, loudly) God protect Austria!

DUKE OF REICHSTADT:

(still reading the first page) God protect France.

(The prayer begins. Religious music. The Curtain falls.)

CURTAIN

ACT III
SCENE 5. THE ROOM IN SCHOENBRUNN

The stage represents the Duke of Reichstadt's room in Schoenbrunn. To the left a large balcony giving on the park, and allowing the city of Vienna to be seen in perspective. A table richly covered on which are two nearly consumed candles. Near the table an arm chair. At the back a sofa. Doors on both sides.

AT RISE, the Duke is seated in the armchair at the left. He holds the book in his hand that he received at the end of the preceding act.

DUKE OF REICHSTADT:

The story of Napoleon Bonaparte! How many triumphs! how much glory! (rising and pacing with agitation as he turns the pages of the little volume) Toulon! Montyenotte! Milesimo! Lodi! Arcole! The Pyramids! Oh! precious book you've just awakened in my soul a thousand unknown ideas! Bonaparte! Bonaparte! It's strange; it seems to me that name arouses vague memories in my mind, confused and bizarre, like the distant echo of lost happiness. Shouts! songs! festivals! old soldiers! pages and this portrait—his! his! (opening the book to the first page and looking at it with emotion) It seems to me this is not the first time he's been seen by me. This story—who gave it to me? and why? especially, why was it hidden from me until today? That name, why was it always mentioned before me only when surrounded by ridiculous lies and slanders? Bonaparte, they told me, a generalissimo of the armies of Louis XVIII and much later, proscribed and exiled by the sovereign like an incompetent and disloyal officer. I've read it. I've read it. It's the history they made me learn in my childhood. And this here—Napoleon, Napoleon. Napoleon, First Consul, Emperor of the French! Napoleon the genius of the century, and the greatest captain of modern times! (his eyes fixed anew on a page of the book) Ah, according to the descriptions of this book, here, right here at Schoenbrunn, a few steps from the throne room, Napoleon's sword, confiscated by the Holy Alliance, is locked in the very room where for many centuries the sword of Charlemagne has been kept, and in this room where I am, the great man reposed the night following the battle of Wagram. (going to the left and partially opening the window) It's there. From this balcony, that he contemplated the Austrian country side of which he was henceforth the master. It's here he received the Emperor, Francis the First, my grandfather, to ask of him the hand of Marie Louise! Who is she then, this Princess of my family who's never been spoken of to me? Who am I, myself? why am I, son of Austria, so violently moved at the thought of all the glories, all the sorrows of France? (here one hears the noise of an orgy off)

SEVERAL VOICES:

(outside) Drink! Drink!

INFANT:

(in a drunken voice) To the health of my dear pupil! To Milord the Duke of Reichstadt. (glasses clink) (gradually getting more drunk) Ah! Caraco! My good José! Long Live the Prime Minister and his excellent wine from Johannesberg.

JOSÉ:

Caraco! Long Live the Prime Minister! Long Live Johannesberg!

INFANT:

To yours, my faithful friend!

JOSÉ:

To yours, my prince.

ALL:

Drink! Drink!

INFANT, JOSÉ AND OTHERS:

(singing in chorus)

Long live orgies
Long live gaiety.
Drinking is freedom.
For tomorrow, perhaps,
We will die.
Snap your fingers at death.
Drink it up, Friends.

(New clinking of glasses, bursts of laughter, then profound silence.)

DUKE OF REICHSTADT:

Now, there's the man they do not blush to give me as a guide, as a master! Ah, the infamous ones! The infamous ones! My head is burning. You might say all the chapters of this marvelous history are coming to life and acting out before me! Bizarre and fantastic visions are rising up everywhere. There, an orgy of drunkenness! As for me, I'm drunk, too. I'm intoxicated with all the great battles, all the shining victories! Marengo! Ulm! Austerlitz, Friedland! Esling! And then, there, always before me, him! him! Napoleon. There he is now in the midst of the ices of Russia! His soldiers fall around him! He remains calm in the midst of these awful disasters, of these incredible sufferings! The thought of his son sustained him, consoled him. His son—who then is this child? What, the son of Napoleon and his name doesn't echo from one end of the earth to the other? Is he, perhaps, dead like his father or a prisoner like me! What became of him? (sitting and turning the pages with agitation) This book is mute! I question it in vain. Nothing. France is invaded. No more family affection! His father embraces him and leaves him forever! His father! Waterloo! Waterloo! Last battle and first defeat! He leaves and, standing on the bridge of the ship, he watches the shores of France disappear. My son, my son, he says, but the ship sails on. And nothing. Nothing at all on the horizon except space and the immensity of the seas. No more palace, no more armies, no more victories! Saint Helena! Saint Helena!

(He falls, overwhelmed, on the couch; the book slips from his hand. A curtain of clouds arises in the distance and disappears. The room in Schoenbrunn, except for where the young man sleeps on the couch, is replaced by the room at Longwood, Saint Helena. A gauze curtain is all that separates the sleeping son from the Father who appears to him.)

ACT III
SCENE 6. THE ROOM AT SAINT HELENA

Napoleon, on his death bed, is surrounded by the historical characters who were present at his last moment.

NAPOLEON:

(to Sir Hudson Lowe) Leave, sir, leave! You've murdered me slowly with premeditation. The infamous Hudson Lowe is made the executor of the high works of the Holy Alliance, and as for me, dying on this frightful rock, far from my family, far from my son, I call on France! I bequeath the opprobrium of my death to the reigning house of England! Leave! (The imperious gesture of the Emperor is repeated by those surrounding him; Lowe leaves; the others press more closely around Napoleon) (pointing to the picture of his son) My friends, if one day you see him, embrace him for me! What have they done to him? Have they even told him I am his father? And what's he think of me, as I die thinking of him! You will tell him, won't you, not to forget he was born French, and never to allow himself to be an instrument in the hands of those who oppress the people of France. All for France and nothing but France! (he visibly weakens and collapses overwhelmed at these last words then, rising in delirium) Desaix! Massina! Run. Charge! they are ours! Head of the Army! France! My son! My son!

(He dies. A scream from all those surrounding him. Hudson Lowe reappears, his watch in his hand. At this point the Duke of Reichstadt, who was very agitated throughout the dream, awakens, letting out a great shout and rushes toward the death bed of Napoleon. But the scene vanishes and resumes its appearance.)

ACT III
SCENE 7

Laughter and the clinking of glasses can be heard.

CHORUS:

(resuming with greater strength)

Long live the orgy.
And gaiety,
Intoxication!— It's freedom.
Tomorrow, perhaps, we shall die.
Defy Death!
Friends, drink up.

ALL:

Drink! Drink!

(At this point, the door to the right opens and The Infant enters, dead drunk, holding two glasses in his hand. Day has come.)

INFANT:

To the health of the student of the most respectable governor of the five parts of the world!

DUKE OF REICHSTADT:

(rushing towards him) Listen and answer.

INFANT:

(offering him one of the two glasses) Do me justice, my prince.

DUKE OF REICHSTADT:

(snatching the glasses from his hand and throwing them out the balcony) Answer, I tell you! (pulling him by force across the stage) The Bonaparte about whom they've told me so many lies—

DON MIGUEL (INFANT):

Ah, History— I'm sleepy, Goodnight. (staggers and falls into an armchair)

DUKE OF REICHSTADT:

The wretch is besotted with drink. (shaking him angrily) Speak, I wish it. Why have they hidden the truth from me?

DON MIGUEL (INFANT):

Why? José is going to answer you. Wake him, José.

DUKE OF REICHSTADT:

You're going to tell me everything. Oh. Get up! Get up!

DON MIGUEL (INFANT):

(waking a little) What do you want from me?

DUKE OF REICHSTADT:

Speak. Who is this Napoleon to me? The Napoleon that I admire, about whose death I weep, and whose memory is henceforth an inseparable part of my life? Who is he?

INFANT:

He's—

DUKE OF REICHSTADT:

Speak, I demand it.

INFANT:

He's your father. (falling motionless at the Duke's feet)

DUKE OF REICHSTADT:

My father! My father! I see clearly in my soul. (covers the portrait with kisses)

(The Curtain falls.)

CURTAIN/BLACKOUT

ACT III
SCENE 8. THE TWO STARS

The stage represents a clearing in a forest near Vienna. Michel Lambert enters as the curtain rises. In his hands he holds two naked swords, which he places at the foot of a tree to the left.

MICHEL LAMBERT:

Wait for me there my little angels! I will be with you in a moment. (he pulls a letter from his pocket and peruses it with fury) "At the clearing in the forest at nine o'clock." I'd prefer to protect a regiment than a young girl. Yesterday morning she swore to me she no longer loved him, that she'd forgotten him for life, and that night at our return from the château, comes, at his direction, a slip of paper from a character with a nasty appearance. I seized it, I paid him his commission in coin worthy of the commission (gesture of giving him a kick) and he left without asking for his tip. I present the letter to Jeanne, who delivers it to me in her turn. We read ten lines, beautiful words, promises, despair, a rendezvous! And there she is, again weeping and lamenting, and is quite ready, I am sure of it, to accept the rendezvous. If I wasn't here to prevent her and take her place! That's if she hasn't followed me this morning! (looking around him) I'm still afraid of that. Those tears, those cursed tears which don't cease. Ah, how I am going to demand an account from him, my little Austrian. How he's soon going to pay me for all the vexations which have tumbled on my back since yesterday! My money, lost, my project gone to the Devil, and above all an unhappy and desolated daughter. Oh, why let him come, let him come then! I need to vent my rage on someone. (he hears nine o'clock ring in the distance) Nine o'clock. (goes to look to the right) At last, it's him! Now, the two of us. (goes to where he placed the swords as the Duke arrives from the path at the right)

DUKE OF REICHSTADT:

(to himself) The hour has struck. Will Jeanne come? Jeanne, on whom alone I place most of my hopes of the future, since they can all be summed up in two words: glory and love.

MICHEL LAMBERT:

(raising his head as he picks up his swords) He talks of love. I'm going to show him some love!

DUKE OF REICHSTADT:

But, shall I reveal to her all the secrets of this strange night? Must I not suspect her father? A soldier, but an Austrian soldier!

MICHEL LAMBERT:

He speaks of Austrians. That suits me. It's been a long while since I had a private conversation with a Kaiserlich. That will revive my hand. (hurling away the swords' scabbards to the left)

DUKE OF REICHSTADT:

She's not coming! No one.

MICHEL LAMBERT:

(showing himself) Indeed. As for me, here I am!

DUKE OF REICHSTADT:

Mathias.

MICHEL LAMBERT:

But it's not me you're expecting, my gentleman.

DUKE OF REICHSTADT:

I admit it. And yet it's never displeasing for me to meet you, my dear Mathias.

MICHEL LAMBERT:

Just a second. I already told you: There's no dear Mathias for you any more. And the proof is: Look.

(presents him the swords)

DUKE OF REICHSTADT:

(shaking) Swords.

MICHEL LAMBERT:

Huh—they frighten you.

DUKE OF REICHSTADT:

(smiling) Fear? Come on. (takes one)

MICHEL LAMBERT:

(aside) Indeed. So young. He's not accustomed to it, and perhaps I will have too great an advantage over him.

DUKE OF REICHSTADT:

What are you saying?

MICHEL LAMBERT:

I am saying that, for you, this is new fruit that one doesn't eat in schools, Mr. Student.

DUKE OF REICHSTADT:

It's true that until today, these weapons and all others have been carefully kept from my hands. Still, my brave fellow, don't worry. At first sight, I feel myself capable of using them.

MICHEL LAMBERT:

I like that better. It pleases me that you say that to me.

DUKE OF REICHSTADT:

Brave Mathias.

MICHEL LAMBERT:

Worthy young man.

DUKE OF REICHSTADT:

Shake.

MICHEL LAMBERT:

I will indeed. That's the way. Shake hands before favoring one with a sword blow.

DUKE OF REICHSTADT:

Huh?

MICHEL LAMBERT:

(putting himself on guard) Are you ready? En garde!

DUKE OF REICHSTADT:

What do you mean?

MICHEL LAMBERT:

En garde! A little lesson in fencing that I mean to give you.

DUKE OF REICHSTADT:

A lesson to me!

MICHEL LAMBERT:

A story to prove to you that I am master in my home, and that my daughter doesn't receive *billets-doux*.

DUKE OF REICHSTADT:

Ah. You know—

MICHEL LAMBERT:

I know everything. Now there's your letter— (tearing it up) That's to tell you, my brave, that we are going to play a rascally role together. Let the devil take courage. Are you ready?

DUKE OF REICHSTADT:

Why, you can't be thinking of it! Me, fight with you?

MICHEL LAMBERT:

Why not?

DUKE OF REICHSTADT:

You, the father of Jeanne?

MICHEL LAMBERT:

It's for that; it's for that very reason. It's because I love her like a father that I am provoking you.

DUKE OF REICHSTADT:

It's for that also, and for that alone, that I refuse.

MICHEL LAMBERT:

You refuse! Indeed, I will force you.

DUKE OF REICHSTADT:

Why are you really very irritated with me?

MICHEL LAMBERT:

I hate you; I hate you to death.

DUKE OF REICHSTADT:

To death! (smiling) That's very grave.

MICHEL LAMBERT:

That's the word. Are you ready?

DUKE OF REICHSTADT:

But my love. Is it such an outrage to Jeanne?

MICHEL LAMBERT:

Yes, an outrage. For she knows quite well, the poor girl, that your family will never stoop to hers.

DUKE OF REICHSTADT:

And why? (placing his sword on a rock; Mathias keeps his) Jeanne is the child of a soldier. And myself, I am nothing else.

MICHEL LAMBERT:

Bah!

DUKE OF REICHSTADT:

Doubtless. My father earned all his rank at the point of his sword. Even yesterday I was unaware of it and that's why I kept silent with Jeanne. But today, at last, I know all about my family and because it is much grander than I had hoped, I would be perjured with the one I love, I would commit a base act because my blood is glorious! Come on, Mathias! You don't believe, you cannot believe it, Mathias, and my heart is revolted at the very thought alone that you will be able to suppose it for a moment.

MICHEL LAMBERT:

(putting his sword down and putting his arms in the arms of the Duke) Then let's talk peacefully. The affair can be arranged. You will have then the consent of your parents?

DUKE OF REICHSTADT:

My parents— (to himself) Those of the court of Austria.

MICHEL LAMBERT:

Well?

DUKE OF REICHSTADT:

For that, and for another thing, it's necessary, perhaps, that I forego a bit their consent.

MICHEL LAMBERT:

He's speaking all for himself alone. A bad sign. (aloud) Look, who are they, these great lords? Name them. And if, on my side, I have no reason for repugnance—

DUKE OF REICHSTADT:

Ah! Name them to you!

MICHEL LAMBERT:

Just simply tell me the name of your father; that will suffice for me.

DUKE OF REICHSTADT:

The name of my father?

MICHEL LAMBERT:

Come on! (aside) I will see if I can pardon him for being Austrian. (aloud) I'm listening.

DUKE OF REICHSTADT:

(aside) Despite the confidence he inspires in me it doesn't go that far.

MICHEL LAMBERT:

I'm still listening.

DUKE OF REICHSTADT:

His name? I won't tell you that.

MICHEL LAMBERT:

Huh?

DUKE OF REICHSTADT:

Impossible.

MICHEL LAMBERT:

Then—you were deceiving me.

DUKE OF REICHSTADT:

Me!

MICHEL LAMBERT:

Your protests just now: phrases, nothing more.

DUKE OF REICHSTADT:

Mathias!

MICHEL LAMBERT:

Like your letters, lies!

DUKE OF REICHSTADT:

Oh! That's too much!

MICHEL LAMBERT:

One of two things. Either you are deceiving me or you blush for him you won't name to me. For your father.

DUKE OF REICHSTADT:

Me! Blush!

MICHEL LAMBERT:

Ah! That warms you up. Come on. I've found the way of getting at you. We will get there. (taking his sword)

DUKE OF REICHSTADT:

My father! My father!

MICHEL LAMBERT:

Name him, if I haven't guessed correctly.

DUKE OF REICHSTADT:

But—

MICHEL LAMBERT:

But, but, but. One doesn't hide that which is honorable! And I declare to you, and I will tell you again a thousand times if necessary, I don't believe it. No, I don't believe in the honor of your father.

DUKE OF REICHSTADT:

(taking up his sword and rushing at Mathias) Ah! Bad luck! Bad luck to you.

MICHEL LAMBERT:

Finally, we are there! And I am, too. (they fight)

DUKE OF REICHSTADT:

(stopping a moment and looking at Michel) An old man.

MICHEL LAMBERT:

A child.

DUKE OF REICHSTADT:

(to himself) If he outraged me! Only me! But him! Him!

MICHEL LAMBERT:

Bah! Perhaps his father was one of those who stole my little Emperor from me.

DUKE OF REICHSTADT:

(putting himself back on guard) I am waiting for you.

MICHEL LAMBERT:

Coming! Coming! (the duel resumes much more violently, Michel pushes a thrust at the Duke's breast and again stops after shouting) Ah, touché! You are wounded, young man.

DUKE OF REICHSTADT:

(smiling) Wounded! Not the least in the world!

MICHEL LAMBERT:

That's astonishing. I really thought—

DUKE OF REICHSTADT:

Indeed, I just felt the iron on my chest (hand on chest) Ah, I'd forgotten. Pardon me, Mathias. The game between us wasn't equal.

MICHEL LAMBERT:

What do you mean?

DUKE OF REICHSTADT:

I mean, I have there, against my heart a talisman which the point of your sword just blunted itself against, and against which it might blunt itself again!

MICHEL LAMBERT:

A talisman!

DUKE OF REICHSTADT:

(removing from his coat the little book he was reading in the previous scene) Yes. This little book; my most precious treasure.

MICHEL LAMBERT:

This book. (takes the book and drops his sword)

DUKE OF REICHSTADT:

And I ask you to take it, and deliver it to Jeanne, if in this duel, Destiny compels me to die!

JEANNE:

(appearing at the back) To die!

DUKE OF REICHSTADT:

Jeanne!

MICHEL LAMBERT:

(looking very emotionally at the Duke) On your knees, my daughter. On your knees before the Emperor Napoleon.

JEANNE:

(kneeling) Son of Napoleon.

(Mathias kneels.)

DUKE OF REICHSTADT:

(surprised) What are you saying, Mathias?

MICHEL LAMBERT:

Mathias! Ah, well, there's no more Mathias here, there's no more Austrians here. Those that you see at your knees, Milord, are two French, two countrymen!

DUKE OF REICHSTADT:

(raising them and pressing them in his arms) French.

MICHEL LAMBERT:

Yes, my prince. Nothing but that. Excuse it is so little. (pointing to himself) Michel Lambert, Lieutenant in the Imperial Guards!

DUKE OF REICHSTADT:

A soldier of the Grand Army.

MICHEL LAMBERT:

Yes, my prince, and hold on. It's my opinion I could not be struck by you anymore than you by me. My little Emperor. I, too, had a talisman against your sword. (opening his German clothes one can see at his neck, the Cross of Honor)

DUKE OF REICHSTADT:

That cross?

MICHEL LAMBERT:

It was he who gave it to me.

DUKE OF REICHSTADT:

Him! The Cross of Honor!

MICHEL LAMBERT:

Now, for the last six weeks I've solicited at the Schoenbrunn palace a wretched situation that your Satanic Austrians refused me with spite, but, at last, yesterday, I succeeded in making you receive that little book.

DUKE OF REICHSTADT:

What! It was you—

MICHEL LAMBERT:

I thought that it would please you. Was I mistaken?

DUKE OF REICHSTADT:

No, no, my brave. So much devotion, love, joy. (pressing Jeanne's hand, then stops and smiles at Michel) Well, your rage a while ago. What's become of it? You allow me to press her hand?

MICHEL LAMBERT:

It's that now I am sure of your honor. I could suspect Frantz, the son of an Austrian gentleman. But I place her under the protection of the son of Napoleon. Poor children, do you realize you've known each other for fourteen years?

BOTH:

Fourteen years!

MICHEL LAMBERT:

Yes, a petition that they addressed to you—

DUKE OF REICHSTADT:

A petition to me!

MICHEL LAMBERT:

Which made us weep like Madeleines, me, and the great Napoleon. Indeed, it was in your name, Milord, that a poor orphan was recommended to your father, The Emperor.

JEANNE:

And your name saved her. That orphan, snatched by you from misery, from death—was me!

DUKE OF REICHSTADT:

You! You! Jeanne!

MICHEL LAMBERT:

So, your two destinies, which Heaven had so long separated, are finally joined. And me, as for me, I can keep both my promises at the same time. To your dying mother, to your father, who separated from you, never to see you again. The poor soldier swore to adopt you; and to spill the last drop of his blood for you.

JEANNE:

My father.

DUKE OF REICHSTADT:

My friend. (Michel presses him to his heart)

MICHEL LAMBERT:

Silence. They're coming to us!

DUKE OF REICHSTADT:

(looking to the right) Ah, my governor. That's fine!

(The Infant, José and men of the Prince's suite enter.)

INFANT:

(bowing) Milord!

DUKE OF REICHSTADT:

That's fine, gentlemen. I will be with you in a moment. (to the Infant) A word, first of all.

INFANT:

I am at your orders, Milord.

DUKE OF REICHSTADT:

I know it. That night's orgy made you my slave. Through you, I know who I am, and the Prime Minister, your protector, would never forgive you for having made me know it.

INFANT:

It's true.

DUKE OF REICHSTADT:

Obey then. You have nothing better to do.

INFANT:

I will obey.

DUKE OF REICHSTADT:

And, first of all, you will obtain from the Prime Minister a situation in the palace for this old man and his daughter.

INFANT:

(aside) I recognize her. (low to Duke) Milord, I will be eager to obey you.

JOSÉ:

(aside, looking at Michel) Heavens! The old bully from the tavern, (covering his face with his hand so as not to be recognized)

DUKE OF REICHSTADT:

(to the people at the back) Come on, gentlemen. Let's leave. (in a low voice) Jeanne, Michel, soon—at Schoenbrunn!

JEANNE AND MICHEL:

At Schoenbrunn.

(The Duke turns towards them as he moves away. The Infant observes the young girl. José avoids Michel. All get ready to leave.)

MICHEL LAMBERT:

(low to Jeanne, watching the Duke) Didn't I say I would recognize him in a thousand? I had only to see him for that.

CURTAIN

ACT IV
SCENE 9. A NEWSPAPER FROM FRANCE

The stage represents a view in the park of Schoenbrunn. There's a party in the palace. The gardens are splendidly illuminated. To the left, the entry to the palace which is reached by a stairway of several steps. A small hill on the horizon dominates the scene. To the right front a rustic pavilion used as living quarters by Michel Lambert and his daughter. The window to the pavilion is lit.

AT RISE, some guests in dominoes promenade in the park. Some lackeys bring refreshments. Music. Everyone hurries into the palace rooms which are closed. Jeanne appears, and takes several steps toward the palace, attracted by the music.

JEANNE:

(on the palace steps) That air, I recognized it. Oh! I've been unable to forget it. It's the one I heard the day of our first meeting. But then he was only Frantz for me, the poor student and my equal! He had eyes only for me. Today, I am alone, far away. I dare hardly look in these brilliant salons, where I cannot, where I must not, be admitted. And does the Duke of Reichstadt give me one thought? It's he, I saw him. How beautiful is that woman! And what dazzling finery. (The waltz stops) The waltz is over, and there he is, always with her. He's talking to her. What's he saying to her? My God! My God! What can he be saying to her? He calls me his sister and I wish to be. Oh, yes, I am happy, I am proud of that title. I am, I am jealous! And despite myself, only seeing him speak to that great lady, my heart is beating to break out of my breast. And the thought of a rival is death! Ah, there he is, at last.

DUKE OF REICHSTADT:

(in black garb; the order of Austria on his breast, the Cross of the Holy Spirit at his throat) Jeanne, my friend! Ah! They kept me from seeing you.

JEANNE:

Milord.

DUKE OF REICHSTADT:

Milord! Jeanne, must you treat me this way? That word in your mouth is like a reproach; a sign of rage or at least pain. Look, in what way am I at fault with you? In what way have I hurt you without knowing it? Answer me!

JEANNE:

It's that— Excuse me, Milord.

DUKE OF REICHSTADT:

Still!

JEANNE:

Mr. Frantz—

DUKE OF REICHSTADT:

Oh. Now there's a gentleman who's one too many. Finally!

JEANNE:

Finally, curiosity attracted me towards these salons. (pointing to the left) During the waltz—

DUKE OF REICHSTADT:

Ah! That waltz. Don't you remember it as I do, as a souvenir?

JEANNE:

It reminds me, making me think at the same time of the beauty of your dancing; the brilliance of her diamonds, and especially that Duchess' crown which shines through the flowers dressing her hair—it reminds me, Milord of the—distance that separates us.

DUKE OF REICHSTADT:

I understand you. You've suffered, Jeanne. And you see, as there's always a little egoism at the bottom of all souls, I am almost happy at that suffering. For it proves to me that, far or near, we always are together and that even the thought, animated as my memory, has a share of your existence, and yours is imperishable in my heart, like the memory of my father.

JEANNE:

And yet, Mr. Frantz, that Duchess—

DUKE OF REICHSTADT:

It's true, I admit it. I was listening with pleasure, even with interest.

JEANNE:

Ah!

DUKE OF REICHSTADT:

She was speaking to me of France.

JEANNE:

And nothing more than France?

DUKE OF REICHSTADT:

I swear to you—

JEANNE:

(with joy) Ah! (aside) All the same, I would like to be the only one to speak to him—

DUKE OF REICHSTADT:

Nothing more. She delivered a newspaper to me that just arrived from Paris.

JEANNE:

From Paris!

DUKE OF REICHSTADT:

Yes, look: there it is. And share my joy, my happiness. Each of these lines is going to speak to me of my country, of my fellow citizens. So, the moment I became the possessor of this treasure, I escaped as fast as I could from the ball to share it with you. Let's read it together.

JEANNE:

Let's read. (they sit down near the hut at right)

DUKE OF REICHSTADT:

(glancing through it quickly and exclaiming) It's strange. Wherever I fix my eyes on this page a single name keeps striking them.

JEANNE:

Indeed! Everywhere! Everywhere! Napoleon!

DUKE OF REICHSTADT:

(reading) "Literature: Two fashionable works are— The History of Napoleon by Mr. de Norvins and especially the Memorial at Saint Helena."

JEANNE:

(reading) "Review of Theatres: One single title shines on all the titles with slight variation: Napoleon Bonaparte, The Emperor! Napoleon or Schoenbrunn and Saint Helena!"

DUKE OF REICHSTADT:

(resuming) "Chamber of Deputies: The chamber voted almost unanimously the law which banned forever" (raising and repeating sadly) "which forever bans the family of Bonaparte from French territories—" (collapsing overwhelmed) Forever.

JEANNE:

God alone is master of the future. But look, look, look farther. "Political Review: A blind government marches forth every day on a false path without ever seeing the ditch into which it is infallibly being dragged to its ruin. The parties are face to face with the name: Napoleon II, circulating amongst the people."

DUKE OF REICHSTADT:

Napoleon II.

JEANNE:

You, Milord! and further on these verses.

DUKE OF REICHSTADT:

These verses?

JEANNE:

It's to you, to you alone they are addressed.

DUKE OF REICHSTADT:

To me?

JEANNE:

Look, rather.

DUKE OF REICHSTADT:

(reading the verses with enthusiasm)

"Courage, child torn from a divine race
You bear on your face your superb origin
All men seeing you recognize in your eyes
A ray eclipsed by the splendor of the Heavens."

MICHEL LAMBERT:

(who's just appeared and heard the last two verses) Bravo! Well done. Who is it said that? What are you reading together, my children?

JEANNE:

Here, here, father. A newspaper from France.

MICHEL LAMBERT:

From France! Excuse me, I am here. As for me, share them! (he is in their midst, pressing the paper in his turn) Ah, by Jove! This is lucky. (reading) "News from Schoenbrunn."

BOTH:

Schoenbrunn!

MICHEL LAMBERT:

"The Duke of Reichstadt, is said to at last know who he is. He learned it from a young and pretty French girl introduced into the castle in the capacity of a simple gardener. She eases the boredom of his captivity for him by speaking to him of his father, of his country, and by giving him the most assiduous care has accustomed him in advance to love the French and particularly the Mamzelles." (Michel stops and resumes several times and the three characters look at each other with indignation and anger)

DUKE OF REICHSTADT:

(exploding) Infamous!

JEANNE:

Father, this is horrible.

DUKE OF REICHSTADT:

This perfidious lie—this cowardly defamation. It's an assassination.

MICHEL LAMBERT:

(extending his hand and embracing Jeanne) Contain yourself. You see, I am calm. I embrace my daughter and I am still proud to press your hand: that tells you how I appreciate the value of these wretched slanders! But one thing. A single result for me from this report. We are already discovered, surrounded by spies and enemies. And I really must press the execution of our plans and put myself into a position to accomplish them this very day.

(At a sign from Michel Lambert, several men in black dominoes, who have just emerged from the salon, come forward and form up on the steps of the palace without being seen by Jeanne or the young man.)

JEANNE AND THE DUKE:

(together) Today!

MICHEL LAMBERT:

Yes, the Prime Minister is giving a masked ball. It's quite right that it be of some use to us. Yes, my children, my good little children of God. Today we are going to sneak out of here and we are going to greet the road to France.

DUKE OF REICHSTADT:

(noticing the dominoes) Imprudent! Be quiet! Don't you see they are leaving the ball and approaching us?

MICHEL LAMBERT:

Those there? Don't be afraid of anything. Good guys. (to Dominoes) Come on, comrades. Say who you are. He will see plainly you are not to be feared.

(The men raise their masks and speak, one after the other. They are the same Bonapartist conspirators who appeared as peasants in Act I.)

FIRST DOMINO:

Pierre Morin, Colonel of Cavalry.

SECOND DOMINO:

Stanislaus Durand, Captain of Marines of the Guard.

THIRD DOMINO:

Jean Verdier, Lieutenant of Staff.

FOURTH DOMINO:

Etienne de Serilly, student at the Polytechnic Institute in 1814.

(They surround the young Duke and he shakes their hands.)

DUKE OF REICHSTADT:

Ah! Frenchmen! Frenchmen! Soldiers of my Father.

MICHEL LAMBERT:

And this sword, which I deliver to your hands, is the one he used at Wagram.

DUKE OF REICHSTADT:

His sword. (he hugs it with respect) My father's sword! The sword of Napoleon! Ah, I will know how to use it; I will fulfill the duty he imposed on me in his last hours. I will draw it from its scabbard only for the glory of France!

MICHEL LAMBERT:

In a short while we will have taken it there.

DUKE OF REICHSTADT:

At last, for me, no more exile, no more proscription. I want only the rights of a simple citizen!

MICHEL LAMBERT:

(with joy) Yes, my little Emperor.

DUKE OF REICHSTADT:

I want to be a soldier, nothing more.

MICHEL LAMBERT:

Yes, my little Emperor! Your father was a corporal! You must indeed begin somewhere. But the time approaches. Let's disperse. Each to his post. Here, my prince, in a few moments we will rejoin each other, after we see a lantern shine at the top of that little hill. (pointing to the hill at the back) That signal will announce to us that the forward guard posts of the Château of Schoenbrunn are ours and that we can leave. (The Duke shakes everyone's hand)

DUKE OF REICHSTADT:

I am waiting for you. (he leaves rapidly to the right)

MICHEL LAMBERT:

A few minutes, not more. Ah, dammit, my children, I am thinking of the Kings of Europe. How their noses will be out of joint.

(Michel Lambert and his friends leave by the left. Jeanne starts to accompany them. Two men in dominoes appear on the palace steps. One of them writes a note in crayon in his notebook, gives it to the other man who returns inside. The first masked man comes to the pavilion and remains masked in the doorway. Jeanne, after having gone some way with her father, returns.)

JEANNE:

(stopping before the masked man) Genius of France protect us! Help, somebody! Who is this man?

THE UNKNOWN:

(removing his mask) Your most sincere and passionate admirer.

JEANNE:

(with fright) You! You, milord!

INFANT:

Could I have had the misfortune of frightening you?

JEANNE:

A great deal! Sire, yes, you make me die of fright, for I see you were there and you heard everything.

INFANT:

Why, I respect the truth too much not to admit it.

JEANNE:

Ah! Pity! Pity! Milord. He's a captive who wants to break his chains; an exile who wants to see his country again. Oh, don't be deaf to my prayers; insensible to my sorrows. This secret you've just surprised. Ah, I conjure you, for mercy's sake, I ask you on my knees. Don't betray him. (she kneels to the Infant)

INFANT:

(aside, looking at her) Beautiful tears! I don't know of a smile that seduces me more. (aloud) Rise, rise, my lovable suppliant, and don't tremble so. They say I'm pitiless, but I'm better than my reputation. And the proof is that I promise you to remain silent. I'll swear it to you if need be.

JEANNE:

Ah, you swear it to me.

INFANT:

(aside) Why not? I am being silent. I already wrote and at this moment José's delivering the message to the Prime Minister that I addressed to him.

JEANNE:

(who has surprised the Infant's smile) Milord, can I believe you?

INFANT:

Eh! What would make you doubt?

JEANNE:

It's that smile. My God! My God! I am trembling again. And yet, you are a gentleman, you are a prince. You couldn't, you wouldn't want to break your word!

INFANT:

Oh! Never and besides, you can without trouble, my child, yourself assure my fidelity to keep my promise.

JEANNE:

How?

INFANT:

By keeping me here, keeping me in sight until the Prince's departure. Oh, only your glance is required to enchain me. Just one, and I will have the greatest pleasure in making myself your prisoner. (goes to her and takes her in his arms)

JEANNE:

(escaping and crying) Stop! Sir, this is unworthy of a Prince. Unworthy of a man of heart. It's cowardice. Leave me alone.

INFANT:

This pride makes you even more beautiful. An added attraction for my love. (he wraps her in his arms) Oh. You belong to me. No one is here to defend you. (pulling her towards the palace) And your father—

JEANNE:

Well? And my father?

INFANT:

He's arrested and, perhaps, at this moment, an Austrian bullet—

(Jeanne utters a scream of terror; Michel Lambert suddenly reappears.)

MICHEL LAMBERT:

Excuse, Majesty, little chap, you lied. I'm still alive. (a light shines on the hill)

JEANNE:

(going to him and throwing herself in his arms) Father!

INFANT:

(aside) José betrayed me.

MICHEL LAMBERT:

I am going to do something so your lie does not become a truth. Release me, daughter. I have an account to settle with that brigand there!

INFANT:

Don't come near me. I am King.

MICHEL LAMBERT:

(picking him up in his arms) And as for me, I am people. Each in his turn.

INFANT:

What are you going to do?

MICHEL LAMBERT:

A good action; an act of justice.

INFANT:

Ah! Caraco!

MICHEL LAMBERT:

There's no "caraco" which will protect you. (Jeanne tries to stop him) Leave me alone, my daughter. A venomous beast, a serpent that I must crush. Don't stop me. (puts the Infant on the ground, his foot on his chest)

INFANT:

Think about it carefully. My life is sacred and my people—

MICHEL LAMBERT:

Who's that? Your people? The Portuguese? You've decided me. What a service I am going to do them.

(He takes him by the throat. The Duke of Reichstadt enters and restrains him.)

DUKE OF REICHSTADT:

What are you going to do? Soil our cause with the death of this man? (The Infant gets loose and rises quickly)

INFANT:

Just in time. (At this moment Austrian soldiers swarm in from all sides and surround the Duke, Michel and Jeanne) Ah— soldiers! Austrian soldiers! José remained faithful to me.

JOSÉ:

(appearing on the left) All is going fine, Majesty. All is going fine.

AN AUSTRIAN GENERAL:

Arrest that man and that young girl. (soldiers surround them)

DUKE OF REICHSTADT:

(drawing his sword) Separate them from me!

GENERAL:

(bowing respectfully) Milord, I am ordered to demand your sword from you.

DUKE OF REICHSTADT:

His sword! Never!

(At this point, on the steps of the palace and dominating the stage, a new person appears, an old man, severely dressed, his breast covered with decorations. Near him, the Abbé Orsini and several court dignitaries. The Duke recoils and utters a shout.)

DUKE OF REICHSTADT:

Ah, the Prime Minister. This sword is my father's. Let Austria kill me if it pretends to take it from me.

PRIME MINISTER:

Milord, I believe you worthy of bearing it! But what His Majesty, The Emperor of Austria, what all the united kings will not suffer is that anyone dare use your name to overthrow the world, and the imprudent friends who've come to give you such ideas must pay dearly for their audacity.

DUKE OF REICHSTADT:

My friends! Great God. Jeanne, Michel. My poor Michel.

PRIME MINISTER:

Austria will determine their destiny.

MICHEL LAMBERT:

Austria! (to Jeanne and the Duke) Ah, my children. You are both lost.

DUKE OF REICHSTADT:

(with despair) Prisoner for life.

INFANT:

José! In less than a month we will be sleeping in the palace at Lisbon.

CURTAIN

ACT V
SCENE 10. THE ILLNESS OF THE COUNTRY

A room in Schoenbrunn, the same as in scene V, except that in the back, there is now Gerard's painting of Napoleon. To the left a couch. To the right an armchair, and another couch as in Scene V at the back.

ARCHDUKE:

Come, come, Doctor, I want to speak to you before shaking the hand of my nephew. He's ill, right? Since I'm permitted to see him again, he's really ill?

DOCTOR:

More than I can tell you, Milord. There are moments when I lose hope.

ARCHDUKE:

Great God!

DOCTOR:

Then sometimes he revives and his eye shines and I force myself to believe that all our cares are not useless! But the mental faculties are too weakened for me to keep my hope for very long. First of all he tried to cheat his boredom by exhausting his strength in his studies and military occupations.

ARCHDUKE:

I understand; he finally knows he has the blood of a soldier in his veins.

DOCTOR:

But the fatigues of this agitated life are killing his body without calming his soul. He cannot tear himself from this devouring activity, and I've taken on myself to ask that, until a new order is established, he be confined to the palace.

ARCHDUKE:

You've done well, doctor, and I thank you for it.

DOCTOR:

Yes, I've done my duty; but recently I've become for him an object of hate and rage.

ARCHDUKE:

Really?

DOCTOR:

(looking to the left) Here he is.

ARCHDUKE:

Him? That's him! How pale he is! Leave me, Doctor. I'll take it upon myself to reconcile you both.

(The Duke enters from the left in the uniform of an Austrian Colonel as the doctor exits right.)

ARCHDUKE:

(going to him) Frantz!

DUKE OF REICHSTADT:

Uncle! At last, I am seeing you again.

ARCHDUKE:

Let me look at you, contemplate you at my leisure. Do you know you are superb that way? That uniform—

DUKE OF REICHSTADT:

Ah! It's not the one I should have preferred to wear.

ARCHDUKE:

(astonished) The Devil! You are difficult; as for me I wear mine well.

DUKE OF REICHSTADT:

You? It's very simple for you! You ought to love Austria.

ARCHDUKE:

I think so, indeed! And you?

DUKE OF REICHSTADT:

Me? Ah! it's impossible! The sword of Napoleon on this white uniform? That is a blasphemy!

ARCHDUKE:

(looking at his own and his nephew's uniform complacently) Well, why, this uniform isn't ugly.

DUKE OF REICHSTADT:

I find it frightful. What do you want? This insipid white is as antipathetic to me as the pale sky of Germany.

ARCHDUKE:

(going to his nephew who has moved away from him bitterly) Come on, shut up! Shut up! As for me, I will advise you; I will distract you; I will teach you the military arts. I will make you a general of our armies.

DUKE OF REICHSTADT:

Oh never! No, never will I serve under the flag of Austria.

ARCHDUKE:

Why not? Austria is somewhat your country?

DUKE OF REICHSTADT:

Not at all!

ARCHDUKE:

(insistent) Indeed so!

DUKE OF REICHSTADT:

Not at all! Not at all! I tell you! And don't ever hope to persuade me of it. Uncle, let's leave that topic. (moving away)

ARCHDUKE:

So be it. You get angry, you get carried away. And you are making yourself sick. By Jove! I didn't return to cause you irritation or boredom. We have at least a joy of softening your troubles. You know who you are and I am no longer obliged to lie when I am with you or to stop myself when I want to praise him to you. (pointing to the portrait of Napoleon)

DUKE OF REICHSTADT:

(coming towards him excitedly) Napoleon, my father.

ARCHDUKE:

Yes; stronger than all of us, that one!

DUKE OF REICHSTADT:

(proudly) Wasn't he?

ARCHDUKE:

And I don't know, if, in antiquity, there was one who was better.

DUKE OF REICHSTADT:

Oh, no.

ARCHDUKE:

The Caesars, the Pompeys, the Scipios. The Hannibals didn't come up to his shoulder.

DUKE OF REICHSTADT:

That's your opinion?

ARCHDUKE:

On honor.

DUKE OF REICHSTADT:

You saw him?

ARCHDUKE:

Yes, yes, Very close up. And I boast of it. He beat me at Wagram.

DUKE OF REICHSTADT:

(enchanted) Beat!

ARCHDUKE:

He wiped the floor with me.

DUKE OF REICHSTADT:

Ah, uncle, my dear uncle, I have to hug you.

ARCHDUKE:

(embracing him) Come on; I was really sure we would end by understanding each other.

DUKE OF REICHSTADT:

(after a silence, falling overwhelmed on to the couch at the left) Napoleon! Napoleon! Yes. I am who I am. And perhaps I am the more unhappy than at the time I was unaware of it. They are enchaining my will, my soul and I am enslaved alive to Schoenbrunn as my father, after so many dazzling acts, was enslaved living at Saint Helena.

ARCHDUKE:

(very moved) My son, my child— Look, dammit, calm down.

DUKE OF REICHSTADT:

Calm down! Is it possible? When they keep me away from all that is dear to me? An angel came to enlighten me, a sweet and pure young girl, whose glance often made me forget all my sorrows. They threw her in a cloister. Never am I permitted to see her again. And her father? A wretched old man; he's rejoined his comrades in the prisons of Schoenbrunn. Despite my prayers, despite my tears. I, the son of Napoleon, I've only got tears to defend those I love!

ARCHDUKE:

My friend, my child, I conjure you—

DUKE OF REICHSTADT:

Jeanne, Michel. My death, perhaps, will set them free.

ARCHDUKE:

Your death!

DUKE OF REICHSTADT:

(rising) Ah, let it come! Let it come!! It's my only wish, my only desire.

ARCHDUKE:

Wretch! Your worst enemies are your thoughts. You will kill yourself, Frantz!

DUKE OF REICHSTADT:

Oh! You might be speaking the truth! (sits right)

ARCHDUKE:

Fool! Am I then less than nothing to you! My friendship? What's the difference, right? What's the difference, that of your grandfather? You're not afraid of breaking our hearts? But do you want? tell me, do you want so as to add to our sorrows that we be accused of this premature death? Do you want to give truth to the slanderous rumors that are spreading and that people are very disposed to believe?

DUKE OF REICHSTADT:

What rumors? What do you mean, uncle?

ARCHDUKE:

They are accusing the court of Austria of lending its hand to an infernal project of the Holy Alliance and causing the son of

Napoleon to die slowly—by poison.

DUKE OF REICHSTADT:

(smiling sadly) By poison.

(The Prime Minister has just appeared in the doorway, having with him the Doctor and the Abbé Orsini.)

PRIME MINISTER AND THE ABBÉ:

Poison!

(Hearing the Prime Minister's voice the Duke rises and goes to lean on the Archduke.)

PRIME MINISTER:

I am strangely surprised, I admit, to hear such a word pronounced by Your Imperial Highness.

ARCHDUKE:

And as for me, I, I say it must be spoken quite loud. To the contrary, to declare boldly and in the face of Europe that the word is a lie!

DUKE OF REICHSTADT:

Poison! No. Those who burden my life are not employing that horrible means to rid themselves of it. No, all the care for me is prodigious, and they watch over my life with solicitude! But the poison which is killing me, which gnaws at me, which must, before long, thrust me into the funereal cellars of the palace, that poison is homesickness. It's the thought of France, of Paris, Paris where I was born and from which I am exiled forever. At last all that my father loved, all that retraces for me the marvels of that grand story! I have conjured my grandfather to make this torture end! He sent me to you, milord. Well, I conjure you, in your turn, to break the chains that keep me here! I need to breathe the air of France, Freedom, Milord, in the name of Heaven, Freedom!

PRIME MINISTER:

(a moment of silence, all eyes are fixed on the Prime Minister; he replies slowly without looking at the other characters) Well, I am going to propose to His Majesty, in the interests of the health of his grandson and to give the lie direct to all these slanders, to authorize the Duke of Reichstadt to leave Schoenbrunn, Vienna and Austria!

(Astonishment by the Abbé, a shout of joy from Frantz, the Archduke and the Doctor who has just reappeared.)

DUKE OF REICHSTADT:

(to himself with joy) Free! I will be free.

ABBÉ ORSINI:

(to himself) What can the Prime Minister be thinking of?

PRIME MINISTER:

But one, one express condition! It's that the Duke of Reichstadt engage, on his word of honor and on the sword of his father, never to approach the soil of France!

ABBÉ ORSINI:

(to himself) I understand.

(The Archduke is sad; the young man is in despair. He sits down without responding.)

PRIME MINISTER:

Are you ready to take that oath?

DUKE OF REICHSTADT:

No, sir.

ARCHDUKE:

Listen, Frantz. They are fighting in Italy! Say one word and I'll lead you there. Come, you'll fight your first battle with me!

DUKE OF REICHSTADT:

(rising) My first battles. Fought against the freedom of peoples. Never.

PRIME MINISTER:

Eh, what. The rest of Europe doesn't suffice for you!

DUKE OF REICHSTADT:

The rest of Europe. And if you were to give me the whole world for exile, I would still choke on it, and I will breathe at ease only in a French village.

PRIME MINISTER:

Still, it seems to me—

DUKE OF REICHSTADT:

(drily) Sir, I will not take either your advice or your remonstrances.

(An officer enters and whispers to the Abbé who gives him some papers.)

ABBÉ ORSINI:

(delivering the papers to the Prime Minister) Excellency, it's done as you wished, and these men have already left Schoenbrunn. (pointing to the balcony) They are all there, ready to leave.

DUKE OF REICHSTADT:

What's all this?

ARCHDUKE:

What's it signify?

PRIME MINISTER:

They are going to transfer to the cells of Vienna all the French that took part in that conspiracy.

DUKE OF REICHSTADT:

(uttering a cry and going to look out the window) Ah! Michel! My old friend. All of them. My brave countrymen. Ah, it's on account of me that they struck you. Pity for them, at least. Pity. Let them be free, if I cannot be.

PRIME MINISTER:

Their fate is in You Highness' hands.

DUKE OF REICHSTADT:

In my hands?

PRIME MINISTER:

Say one word and I will see to it that they are escorted across the frontiers of the Empire.

DUKE OF REICHSTADT:

One word?

PRIME MINISTER:

Don't you understand me? Perhaps you will do for them, what you refuse to our solicitations and the prayers of your uncle.

DUKE OF REICHSTADT:

Ah, I understand you, sir. And I am conjured, I give up. To those who devoted their lives to me, I owe sacrifice for sacrifice. (with effort) Well, let them be permitted to leave Austria, let them go. In my name salute the heavens of home. And as for me, I only want to see them and press their hands one last time before their departure. And I promise, (drawing his sword) I swear, on the sword of my father, I will never set foot on the soil of France.

(The sword falls from his hands and he falls annihilated on the couch. The Archduke and the Doctor hover over him.)

ARCHDUKE:

Frantz.

DOCTOR:

I tremble.

DUKE OF REICHSTADT:

(coming to, and placing his hand, first to his face, then to his chest) How can I bear this? this supreme farewell to my country. Is it my heart that's breaking? Is my soul leaving me?

PRIME MINISTER:

(approaching him and bowing) Give the order, milord. I am yours and I will keep my promise.

DUKE OF REICHSTADT:

Come, sir, Uncle, that oath was my death warrant.

(The Duke leaves leaning on the Doctor; the Prime Minister and the Abbé follow them.)

ARCHDUKE:

(alone) His death warrant! Is it possible, great gods! Will it be consummated so soon, this horrible work of European policy? The Kings have extended their hands to the Infant of Portugal. As the reward for the freedom of the Duke of Reichstadt, they sold him the crown, they supported him, confirmed him in his usurpation; he reigns at last, in scorn of all law divine and human. While those who wished to make his student— Oh, but I don't want to despair yet, My God, of your justice. No, you don't want to snatch him from my tenderness. No, I will convince him to follow me. I will succeed by triumphing over his thoughts, his memories, perhaps. (looking out the window) There he is under the balcony. He can smile again. And he's raising his head. You'd say that an instant of happiness— Ah, it's because he's near one of them, that Frenchman, that his voice has set free. My wishes are accomplished already. He's forgotten his sadness and we will save him. We will save him!

(The Duke returns smiling, leaning on Michel Lambert's arm. Michel has resumed French uniform. Very simple. His Cross of Honor on his breast. They seem to be continuing a conversation and are followed by pages and officers of the palace. The Duke is smiling, but speaking with great difficulty.)

DUKE OF REICHSTADT:

Come, my friend. My old comrade continues to speak to me of my father. Come, I'll be better this way, listening to you and seeing him. (with the assistance of Michel and the Doctor he sits on the couch so he can look at the Emperor's picture)

ARCHDUKE:

Frantz.

DUKE OF REICHSTADT:

(extending his hand to him) Ah, uncle, I am much better now, much better. (the Archduke shows joy)

DOCTOR:

(low to Archduke) Lost! This last trial has destroyed his strength and his life.

ARCHDUKE:

Heavens!

(The Duke has a fit of light coughing which appears to cause him to suffer greatly. The cough is repeated throughout the scene at intervals.)

MICHEL LAMBERT:

(giving a military salute to the Archduke) My general!

ARCHDUKE:

(to himself, drying his eyes) Poor victim! dear victim!

MICHEL LAMBERT:

(low) You're crying—

ARCHDUKE:

(low) Me? Not at all, but yourself?

MICHEL LAMBERT:

(low) Not at all, my general, not at all.

ARCHDUKE:

(low) Ah, we understand each other, my brave. Your hand, your hand!

MICHEL LAMBERT:

Ah, my general. Sonofabitch. As for you, you are Austrian.

Only, you're not. (they shake hands)

ARCHDUKE:

Silence for him!

MICHEL LAMBERT:

That's right. Mum's the word.

DUKE OF REICHSTADT:

(who's been resting, contemplating the portrait) Well, you aren't telling me anything, Michel, and still I'm listening.

ARCHDUKE:

Speak, speak, my brave. (the two go to the Duke)

DUKE OF REICHSTADT:

You'd begun the story of a terrible battle. Continue it. Listening to you, I am forgetting.

MICHEL LAMBERT:

Moscow! Terrible, yes, you said it; and it's you who won it without any doubt of it, Milord.

DUKE OF REICHSTADT:

(smiling) Me!

MICHEL LAMBERT:

Yourself! You weren't yet a year old. But it's still a fact. Yours was the victory. It's your father's portrait which just made me recall it. The morning of the great battle, Napoleon, in the midst of Russian ice, surrounded by a discouraged and dying army, received from Paris the portrait of his son. After having looked at it for a time, as you are looking at his right now, Milord, he showed it to all the soldiers who came to embrace it along with him. As for me, I was there, I was there, do you see? from that moment there was no ice, no hunger, no misery; Hope returned to us with courage and the remnant of the Grand Army once again obtained a dazzling victory, reviving to the shouts of Long Live The Emperor! Long Live the King of Rome!

(At this shout everyone turns towards Lambert, but at a sign from the Archduke are silent.)

ARCHDUKE:

Very imprudent! Would you quiet down! If others were to hear you.

MICHEL LAMBERT:

(low) That's true. That would singe their ears! That won't happen again. They will separate me from him once more, perhaps, and I will never be able to speak to him again about his father.

ARCHDUKE:

Well, Frantz, my child?

DUKE OF REICHSTADT:

(slowly raising his head, looking fixedly at his uncle and saying with a sad smile) The King of Rome. The Church predicted at my birth that the title would bring me misfortune.

DOCTOR:

(who had momentarily disappeared, to the Duke) Milord, the ladies of honor to Her Imperial Highness, The Duchess Sophie.

DUKE OF REICHSTADT:

I am ready to receive them!

(The ladies of honor, then Jeanne, followed by several nuns having the Mother Superior of their Convent at their head. At this entry the ladies of Honor all bow. Michel Lambert has placed himself near the door and utters a cry)

MICHEL LAMBERT:

What do I see? My daughter Jeanne!

DOCTOR:

(low to Michel) Silence! You are going to understand everything. I've tried to deceive him about his condition. Let's leave him this last illusion; he's had so few in his life.

JEANNE:

(in the dress of a novice) Father.

DUKE OF REICHSTADT:

(rushing to her) Jeanne!

JEANNE:

(between him and Michel) Myself, Milord. (offering one hand to Michel, the other to the Duke)

DUKE OF REICHSTADT:

(with emotion) My sister!

JEANNE:

I am going to take the veil, Milord, under the protection of Madame The Archduchess; she allowed me while returning to the abbey of Saint Theresa near the palace where I must take my vows, to be escorted near my father, near you. At this supreme moment, she who enters forever into the cloister is going to die to the world, and she's coming, custom demands it, to ask her family and her friends to repeat with her, and for her, the last prayer pronounced for the dying! (general emotion)

DUKE OF REICHSTADT:

(with bitterness) The dying!

JEANNE:

(looking in turn from Michel to the Duke) My only family and my only friends. There they are. Will you, milord, will you do me this sad and final office that I come to implore of your affection for me?

DUKE OF REICHSTADT:

(with profound sadness) Nothing for me in this life! Nothing! Neither glory! (looking at Jeanne) Nor happiness! (stretching his hand to the young girl) Thanks, Jeanne, thanks for having thought of me.

(The pages bring velour cushions to the front of the stage. The Duke kneels with effort, supported by the Archduke, Jeanne kneels near him. Everyone kneels. Devout silence.)

JEANNE:

(praying) Lord, from the depth of the Abyss, the shout of your silence has risen to you! Lord have pity.

DUKE OF REICHSTADT:

Have pity.

ALL:

(in a low voice) Have pity.

DUKE OF REICHSTADT:

(praying) Holy angels of Heaven! Pray! My strength is exhausted; my days are shortened. I have not sinned and yet my eyes see only enemies who ceaselessly plot some device to ruin me. They told me that the night I am in will change to a day of light! But when I waited, even until morning the tomb will be my house and I will have no other bed than this place of shadows! Holy angels of Heaven! Pray! Pray for those who love the one who's calling you to yourself. Pardon those who hate you. Holy angels of Heaven, support the unfortunate, treasures of fidelity, pray!

JEANNE:

(praying) Angels of Heaven, pray.

ALL:

Pray!

(During this prayer the young girl has been very moved; the Duke has gradually weakened. They rise.)

JEANNE:

(rising) Milord! My father! From this moment I belong to God. (she leaves with the nuns)

DUKE OF REICHSTADT:

And as for me, I belong to death!

(He falls on the couch. Everyone surrounds him. The Archduke and Michel Lambert shed tears.)

MICHEL LAMBERT:

What are you saying, Milord?

ARCHDUKE:

My Frantz, my child, separate yourself from this horrible thought.

DUKE OF REICHSTADT:

(very weak) It's on myself, I know, on myself alone, they've just pronounced that prayer.

ARCHDUKE:

(weeping) Frantz!

MICHEL LAMBERT:

Milord!

DUKE OF REICHSTADT:

(dying) Why weep, my uncle? And you, my old Michel, and you all, my friends, why are you crying? See if I am crying! I am happy at last, really happy. When I am marching towards him, my friends, no more tears. And you, Michel, a bit of courage still. Help me to die, head high, and with a smile on my lips. Separate from me the thought of what I would have been able to do by telling me what he had done!

MICHEL LAMBERT:

(weeping) Well, Milord, the 23rd of January, 1814, he learned that foreigners had just set foot in France and once again he was going to put himself on campaign.

(Jeanne and the nuns return from the left quietly. Jeanne, a black veil on her white robe, comes forward weeping and approaches her father who takes her hand and pursues his tale.)

MICHEL LAMBERT:

(continuing) His son was sleeping before his eyes. And as he ordered the preparations for the new war, The Emperor kissed the face of the sleeping child and repeated sadly, "I will never see him again. Never! Never! Father and son will never be reunited."

DUKE OF REICHSTADT:

(smiling) Oh, you were mistaken, father. Reunited by death! Here I am father, I am coming to you. Here I am.

(Falls back dead on the couch. All the characters utter a cry and place themselves on their knees. Clouds envelop the stage.)

EPILOGUE
SCENE 11. THE ETERNAL CITY

When the clouds have disappeared, one perceives Heaven and the Eternal city. Napoleon surrounded by his braves casts, from the height of the Heaven, his glance toward the Earth which appears in the distance in the midst of space and detaches itself from a fiery horizon. The Emperor awaits his son. All his old generals, his officers and his soldiers share his anxiety and his emotion.

EPILOGUE
SCENE XII

The Harp resounds everywhere. An eagle, wings outspread and holding in its talons broken chains, rises above the ball of the world. And the son of the Emperor, standing and pressing against his heart his father's sword, slowly climbs toward Heaven, extending his arms to Napoleon and presenting him the weapon he holds in his hand. They are finally reunited with each other. All the old soldiers kneel. The standards wave. A dazzling music plays as the curtain falls.

CURTAIN

ABOUT THE AUTHOR

Frank J. Morlock has written and translated many plays since retiring from the legal profession in 1992. His translations have also appeared on Project Gutenberg, the Alexandre Dumas Père web page, Literature in the Age of Napoléon, Infinite Artistries.com, and Munsey's (formerly Blackmask). In 2006 he received an award from the North American Jules Verne Society for his translations of Verne's plays. He lives and works in México.

www.ingramcontent.com/pod-product-compliance
Lightning Source LLC
LaVergne TN
LVHW041620070426
835507LV00008B/366